THE
STRATEGY
OF SATAN

The Strategy of Satan

HOW TO DETECT AND DEFEAT HIM

Warren W. Wiersbe

Tyndale House
Publishers, Inc.
Wheaton, Illinois

These studies
originally appeared in
another form in my
book *Creative
Christian Living*. I
want to thank the
publishers, Fleming H.
Revell Company, for
permitting me to adapt
the material for this
present book.

All Bible quotations
are from *The New
American Standard
Bible*, unless
otherwise indicated.

Library of Congress Catalog Card Number 79-63647.
ISBN 0-8423-6665-2.
21 22 23 24 25 93

To the memory of
PETER DEYNEKA, SR.

CONTENTS

INTRODUCTION
What This Book Is About And How You Should Use It

This book is about Satan and the strategy he has to wreck your Christian life and (if possible) destroy you.

Four persons in the Old Testament had a direct confrontation with Satan. From their experiences we will learn

the targets *Satan aims at in your life;*
the weapons *he uses to attack you;*
the purposes *that he wants to achieve; and*
the defenses *God has provided for you.*

Please keep in mind that this book is a manual of arms for the Christian soldier. It is not a devotional reader for the believer who has gone AWOL. It is a deadly serious guidebook for the dedicated Christian who is on the battlefield and wants to know how to win.

Please do not speed-read these pages. Read them carefully, especially the many quotations from God's Word. Ask the Holy Spirit to help you understand and assimilate these truths. There is no "padding" in these chapters. These studies represent the essentials—the rock-bottom fundamentals—of what God has taught me about the Christian warfare through many years of studying and battling. I have proved these truths in my own life and ministry.

No doubt Satan will do everything he can to keep you from benefiting from this book. He will distract you and detour you. He will seek to confuse you, or perhaps make you critical. He will arrange interruptions. I suggest you ask the Lord for his help and protection as you study these pages. "Greater is He who is in you than he who is in the world" (1 John 4:4). *Positionally*, you are in Christ and delivered from the power of Satan.

> *For He delivered us from the domain of darkness, and transferred us to the kingdom of His beloved Son.* Colossians 1:13

My aim in this book is to help you experience this victory *practically*.

The truths in these pages will do you no good unless they are put into practice. Satan enjoys seeing Christians get a head-knowledge of victory without a heart-experience, because this lulls believers into a false security, and Satan finds them an easy prey. It is not the *reading* of truth, or even the *enjoying* of truth that brings the blessing. It is the *doing* of the truth. Therefore, determine with the Spirit's help to put these truths into practice.

Remember: you are not fighting *for* victory, but *from* victory, for Jesus Christ has already defeated Satan!

> *When He had disarmed the rulers and authorities* [Satanic powers], *He made a public display of them, having triumphed over them through Him* [Christ]. Colossians 2:15

> *Now judgment is upon this world; now the ruler of this world shall be cast out.* John 12:31

> *And they overcame him* [Satan] *because of the blood of the Lamb and because of the word of their testimony, and they did not love their life even to death.* Revelation 12:11

Now, on to victory!

ONE
The
Deceiver

"He was a murderer from the beginning, and does not stand in the truth, because there is no truth in him. Whenever he speaks a lie, he speaks from his own nature; for he is a liar, and the father of lies."
John 8:44

And the great dragon was thrown down, the serpent of old who is called the devil and Satan, who deceives the whole world. Revelation 12:9

But I am afraid, lest as the serpent deceived Eve by his craftiness, your minds should be led astray from the simplicity and purity of devotion to Christ. 2 Corinthians 11:3

For many deceivers have gone out into the world. 2 John 7

Now the serpent was more crafty than any beast of the field which the Lord God had made. And he said to the woman, "Indeed, has God said, 'You shall not eat from any tree of the garden'?"
   And the woman said to the serpent, "From the fruit of the trees of the garden, we may eat; but from

the fruit of the tree which is in the middle of the garden, God has said, 'You shall not eat from it or touch it, lest you die.' "

And the serpent said to the woman, "You surely shall not die! For God knows that in the day you eat from it your eyes will be opened, and you will be like God, knowing good and evil."

When the woman saw that the tree was good for food, and that it was a delight to the eyes, and that the tree was desirable to make one wise, she took from its fruit and ate; and she gave also to her husband with her, and he ate.

Then the eyes of both of them were opened, and they knew that they were naked; and they sewed fig leaves together and made themselves loin coverings. Genesis 3:1-7

1. SATAN'S TARGET—YOUR MIND

When Satan wanted to lead the first man and woman into sin, he started by attacking the woman's mind. This is made clear in 2 Corinthians 11:3.

> But I am afraid, lest as the serpent deceived Eve by his craftiness, your minds should be led astray from the simplicity and purity of devotion to Christ.

Why would Satan want to attack your mind? Because your mind is the part of the image of God where God communicates with you and reveals his will to you. It is unfortunate that some Christians have minimized the significance of the mind, because the Bible emphasizes its importance.

Do not lie to one another, since you have laid aside the old self with its evil practices, and have put on the new self who is being renewed to a true knowledge according to the image of the One who created him. Colossians 3:9, 10

This I say therefore, and affirm together with the Lord, that you walk no longer just as the Gentiles also walk, in the futility of their mind, being darkened in their understanding, excluded from the life of God, because of the ignorance that is in them, because of the hardness of their heart; and they, having become callous, have given themselves over to sensuality, for the practice of every kind of impurity with greediness. But you did not learn Christ in this way, if indeed you have heard Him and have been taught in Him, just as truth is in Jesus, that, in reference to your former manner of life, you lay aside the old self, which is being corrupted in accordance with the lusts of deceit, and that you be renewed in the spirit of your mind, and put on the new self, which in the likeness of God has been created in righteousness and holiness of the truth. Ephesians 4:17-24

And do not be conformed to this world, but be transformed by the renewing of your mind, that you may prove what the will of God is, that which is good and acceptable and perfect. Romans 12:2

God renews our lives by renewing our minds, and he renews our minds through his truth. This truth is the Word of God.

> *Sanctify them in the truth; Thy word is truth.*
> John 17:17

If Satan can get you to believe a lie, then he can begin to work in your life to lead you into sin. This is why he attacks the mind, and this is why we must protect our minds from the attacks of the wicked one.

> *Finally, brethren, whatever is true, whatever is honorable, whatever is right, whatever is pure, whatever is lovely, whatever is of good repute, if there is any excellence and if anything worthy of praise, let your mind dwell on these things.* Philippians 4:8

"If it is not true," Paul writes, "do not let it enter your mind."

In recent years, science has discovered many fascinating things about the human mind. Like a computer, your mind can store facts and impressions—and even emotions—and recall them years later. Your mind can reach into the past through memory, or it can reach into the future through imagination. Your thinking affects your feeling and your willing.

> *For as he thinks within himself, so he is.*
> Proverbs 23:7

The doctor says, "You are what you eat." The psychologist says, "You are what you think."

Satan knows the tremendous power of your mind, and he tries to capture it for himself.

> The steadfast of mind Thou wilt keep in perfect peace, because he trusts in Thee.
> Isaiah 26:3

> For the mind set on the flesh is death, but the mind set on the Spirit is life and peace.
> Romans 8:6

Your mind affects your whole being. While I do not totally agree with the "success psychology" and "healing psychology" of our day, I must admit that attitudes are important to health and success in life. The exciting new field of "holistic medicine" draws upon the influences of the mind to help the patient cure himself. Sales managers "psych up" their salesmen with thoughts of accomplishment and success, just as coaches do their football teams. While thinking alone does not make it so, it certainly helps!

2. SATAN'S WEAPON—LIES

Satan came to Eve as the serpent, the subtle deceiver.

> . . . the serpent of old who is called the devil and Satan, who deceives the whole world.
> Revelation 12:9

> . . . there is no truth in him . . . for he is a liar and the father of lies. John 8:44

It is important that you notice the steps Satan took in getting Eve to believe his lie.

(1) *He questioned God's Word.* "Indeed, has God said . . . ?" He did not deny that God had spoken; he simply questioned whether God had really said what Eve thought he had said. "Perhaps you misunderstood what God spoke," is Satan's suggestion. "You owe it to yourself to rethink what he said." It is worth noting that in this suggestion Satan is also questioning God's goodness. "If God really loved you, he wouldn't keep something from you." He tried the same approach with our Lord in the wilderness: "If you are God's beloved Son, why are you hungry?"

(2) *He denied God's Word.* "You surely shall not die!" It is but a short step from questioning God's Word to denying it. Of course, neither Adam nor Eve had ever seen death. All they had to go on was the Word of God, *but this was all they needed.* If Eve had not listened to Satan questioning God's Word, she would never have fallen into his trap when he denied God's Word.

(3) *He substituted his own lie.* "You will be like God!" Adam and Eve were already made in the image of God, but Satan tempted them with an even greater privilege: to be like God! This was, of course, Satan's great ambition when he was Lucifer, God's angelic servant.

"How you have fallen from heaven, O star of the morning, son of the dawn! You have been cut down to the earth, you who have weakened the nations! But you said in your heart, 'I will ascend to heaven; I will raise my throne above the stars of God, and I will sit on the mount of the assembly, in the

20

recesses of the north. I will ascend above the heights of the clouds; I will make myself like the Most High.' " Isaiah 14:12-14

Satan is a created being, a creature; but he wanted to be worshiped and served like the Creator. It was this attitude that led him to rebel against God and seek to establish his own kingdom. "You will be like God" is the one gigantic lie that has controlled civilization since the fall of man.

For they exchanged the truth of God for a lie [literally "the lie"], *and worshiped and served the creature rather than the Creator, who is blessed forever. Amen.* Romans 1:25

Satan desires worship and service, and Jesus Christ would give him neither!

Again, the devil took Him to a very high mountain, and showed Him all the kingdoms of the world, and their glory; and he said to Him, "All these things will I give You, if You fall down and worship me." Then Jesus said to him, "Begone, Satan! For it is written, 'You shall worship the Lord your God, and serve Him only.' " Matthew 4:8-10

Satan's lie "You will be like God" motivates and controls much of our civilization today. Man is seeking to pull himself up by his own bootstraps. He is working to build a utopia on earth and possibly take it to outer space. Through education, psychiatry, religions of one kind or another (most of which ignore Jesus Christ, sin, and salvation), and better environment, men are defying God and deifying themselves. They are playing right into the hands of Satan.

How did Eve respond to Satan's approach? She responded by making three mistakes that led her into sin.

(1) *She took away from God's Word.* In verse 2, Eve omitted the word "freely." God's original word in Genesis 2:16 was, "From any tree of the garden you may eat freely." We get the impression that Eve caught Satan's subtle suggestion, "God is holding out on you!" When you start to question or forget the grace of God and the goodness of God, you will find it much easier to disobey the will of God.

(2) *She added to God's Word.* We do not find the words "or touch it" in God's original command. They may have been there, but they are not in the record. Not only did Eve make God's original word *less gracious* by omitting the word "freely," but she also made the commandment *more grievous* by adding "or touch it." "His commandments are not burdensome" (1 John 5:3). Satan wants us to believe they are burdensome, and that he has something better to offer.

(3) *She changed God's Word.* God did not say, "Lest you die." He said, "For in the day that you eat from it you shall surely die" (Genesis 2:17). The penalty for disobedience as presented by the enemy did not seem as harsh; therefore, Eve could consider forsaking God's will and obeying Satan's will.

Once you have treated God's Word in this fashion, you are wide open for the devil's final trick. He merely permitted Eve to consider the tree *apart from God's Word*. "Get a good look at it! See it as it really is!" It was "good for food ... a delight to the eyes ... desirable to make one wise" (Genesis 3:6). She had to make a choice: God's Word or Satan's word? She rejected God's Word, believed Satan, and sinned. You and I have been suffering from the consequences of her decision, as has the whole human race.

God accomplishes his will on earth through *truth*; Satan accomplishes his purposes through *lies*. When the child of God believes God's truth, then the Spirit of God can work in power; for the Holy Spirit is "the Spirit of truth" (John 16:13). But when a person believes a lie, then Satan goes to work in that life; "for he is a liar, and the father of lies" (John 8:44). Faith in God's truth leads to victory; faith in Satan's lies leads to defeat.

However, Satan never advertises, "This is a lie!" He is the serpent, the deceiver, and he always masquerades his lies as God's truth.

> *For such men are false apostles, deceitful workers, disguising themselves as apostles of Christ. And no wonder, for even Satan disguises himself as an angel of light.* 2 Corinthians 11:13, 14

Satan did not approach Eve in his true nature; he masqueraded by using the serpent. Satan is a counterfeiter, an imitator.

There are *counterfeit Christians*.

> ... *dangers among* false brethren. 2 Corinthians 11:26

". . . the tares are the sons of the evil one."
Matthew 13:38

"You are of your father *the devil."* John 8:44

There is *a counterfeit gospel*.

> *But even though we, or an angel from heaven,*
> *should preach to you a gospel contrary to that*
> *which we have preached to you, let him be*
> *accursed.* Galatians 1:8

There are counterfeit *ministers of the gospel*.

> *. . . for even Satan disguises himself as an*
> *angel of light. Therefore it is not surprising if*
> his servants *also disguise themselves as ser-*
> *vants of righteousness.* 2 Corinthians 11:14, 15

There is a *counterfeit righteousness*.

> *For not knowing about God's righteousness,*
> *and seeking to establish their own, they did*
> *not subject themselves to the righteousness of*
> *God.* Romans 10:3

There is even a counterfeit *"church of Satan."*

> *I know your tribulation and your poverty*
> *(but you are rich), and the blasphemy by*
> *those who say they are Jews* [i.e., God's people]
> *and are not, but are* a synagogue of Satan.
> Revelation 2:9

And this counterfeit church has *counterfeit*
doctrines.

> *But the Spirit explicitly says that in later*
> *times some will fall away from the faith,*

paying attention to deceitful spirits and doctrines of demons. 1 Timothy 4:1

All of this will end, of course, in the appearance
of *a counterfeit Christ*—the Antichrist—who
will accept for Satan the worship and service of
the whole world.

> *And then that lawless one will be revealed.
> . . . the one whose coming is in accord with
> the activity of Satan, with all powers and
> signs and false wonders, and with all the
> deception of wickedness for those who
> perish.* 2 Thessalonians 2:8-10

> *And all who dwell on the earth will worship
> him.* Revelation 13:8

Satan's target is your mind, and his weapon is
lies. What is his purpose?

3. SATAN'S PURPOSE—
TO MAKE YOU IGNORANT OF GOD'S WILL

Satan attacks God's Word because God's Word
reveals God's will.

> *Thy word is a lamp to my feet, and a light to
> my path.* Psalm 119:105

> *I delight to do Thy will, O my God; Thy Law
> is within my heart.* Psalm 40:8

Apart from the Word of God, we have no sure
understanding of the will of God. The will of God
is the expression of God's love for us.

The counsel of the Lord stands forever, the plans of his heart *from generation to generation.* Psalm 33:11

God's will comes from God's heart. It is not an impersonal thing, but a very personal matter with the Lord. He has a personal understanding of each of his children—their natures, their names, their needs—and he tailors his plans accordingly.

God wants us to *know* his will.

"The God of our fathers has appointed you to know His will." Acts 22:14

He also wants us to *understand* his will.

So then do not be foolish, but understand *what the will of the Lord is.* Ephesians 5:17

He wants this understanding of his will to *fill us* and *control us.*

We have not ceased to pray for you and to ask that you may be filled with the knowledge of His will in all spiritual wisdom and understanding. Colossians 1:9

The result of all this is the believer

doing the will of God *from the heart.* Ephesians 6:6

God's will is not a duty; it is a delight. The Christian delights to discover the will of God and then obey from the heart. The will of God is his nourishment.

"My food is to do the will of Him who sent Me, and to accomplish His work." John 4:34

You and I must pray (as did Epaphras) that we

> *may stand perfect and fully assured in all the will of God.* Colossians 4:12

If Satan can make you ignorant of God's will, he will rob you of all the glorious blessings God has planned for your life. You will make bad decisions, get involved in sinful activities, and build the wrong kind of life. And, sad to say, *you will influence others to go wrong!* In my ministry of the Word in many places, I have seen the tragic consequences of lives out of the will of God.

Christians who are ignorant of God's will lose the enjoyment of God's peace and power. They cannot grow into their full potential, nor can they accomplish what God has planned for them. Instead of traveling first-class, they travel second- or third-class, complaining all the way. They live like paupers because they have cut themselves off from God's great wealth. They spend their lives—even worse, they *waste* their lives—when they could be *investing* their lives.

> *But the one who does the will of God abides forever.* 1 John 2:17

4. YOUR DEFENSE—
THE INSPIRED WORD OF GOD

Only the inspired Word of God can reveal and defeat the devil's lies. You cannot reason with Satan, nor (as Eve discovered) can you even safely converse with him. Man's wisdom is no match for Satan's cunning. Our only defense is the inspired Word of God.

It was this weapon that our Lord used when he was tempted by Satan in the wilderness.

Then Jesus was led up by the Spirit into the wilderness to be tempted by the devil. And after He had fasted forty days and forty nights, He then became hungry. And the tempter came and said to Him, "If You are the Son of God, command that these stones become bread."

But He answered and said, "It is written, 'Man shall not live on bread alone, but on every word that proceeds out of the mouth of God.'"

Then the devil took Him into the holy city; and he stood Him on the pinnacle of the temple, and said to Him, "If You are the Son of God throw Yourself down; for it is written, 'He will give His angels charge concerning You; and on their hands they will bear You up, lest You strike Your foot against a stone.'"

Jesus said to him, "On the other hand, it is written, 'You shall not tempt the Lord your God.'"

Again, the devil took Him to a very high mountain, and showed Him all the kingdoms of the world, and their glory; and he said to Him, "All these things will I give You, if You fall down and worship me."

Then Jesus said to him, "Begone, Satan! For it is written, 'You shall worship the Lord your God, and serve Him only.'"

Then the devil left Him; and behold, angels came and began to minister to Him. Matthew 4:1-11

Our Lord did not use his divine power to defeat Satan. He used the same weapon that is available to us today: the Word of God. Jesus was led by the Spirit of God and filled with the Word of God. As we shall see in a later chapter, the Word of God is "the sword of the Spirit" (Ephesians 6:17); and the Holy Spirit can enable us to wield that sword effectively. If you and I are going to defeat Satan's lies, we must depend on the Word of God. This fact lays several responsibilities upon us.

(1) *We must know God's Word.* There is no reason why any believer should be ignorant of his Bible. The Word of God is available to us in many translations. We have the Holy Spirit within us to teach us the truths of the Word (John 16:13-15). There are a multitude of Bible study helps available. We can turn on the radio and listen to excellent preachers and Bible teachers expound God's Word. In local churches, there are pastors and teachers who minister the Word; and in many areas, there are seminars and Bible study groups for further study. If an intelligent believer today does not know his Bible, it is his or her own fault!

This means, of course, taking time to *read* and *study* the Bible. No one will master God's Word in a lifetime of study, but we should learn all we can. We must *make* time, not "find time," to read and study the Word of God. Just as a machinist studies the shop manual, and the surgeon studies his medical texts, so the Christian must study the Word of God. Bible study is not a luxury; it is a necessity.

(2) *We must memorize God's Word.* Our Lord

did not have a concordance with him in the wilderness! He reached back into the Books of Moses, selected Deuteronomy, and quoted three verses from that book to silence Satan. Most adults think that Bible memorization is for children in Sunday school, when actually it is for *every believer*. Adult Christians need the Word far more than the children do, although it is good for children to memorize God's Word.

> *Thy word I have treasured in my heart, that I may not sin against Thee.* Psalm 119:11

> *The law of his God is in his heart; his steps do not slip.* Psalm 37:31

> *I delight to do Thy will, O my God; Thy Law is within my heart.* Psalm 40:8

If you do not have a systematic Bible memory program, get one started. Your pastor can give you counsel and no doubt provide materials for you. Check your local Christian bookstore for Bible memory helps.

(3) *We must meditate on God's Word.* Meditation is to the inner man what digestion is to the outer man. If you did not digest your food, you would sicken and die.

> *This book of the law shall not depart from your mouth, but you shall meditate on it day and night, so that you may be careful to do according to all that is written in it; for then you will make your way prosperous, and then you will have success.* Joshua 1:8

But his delight is in the law of the Lord, and in His law he meditates day and night. Psalm 1:2

Do you sincerely *delight* in the Word of God, or do you read it only out of duty? Do you rush through your "morning devotions," or take time to feed on God's truth? Measure yourself by these statements by the psalmist:

How sweet are Thy words to my taste! Yes, sweeter than honey to my mouth! Psalm 119:103

I rise before dawn and cry for help; I wait for Thy words. My eyes anticipate the night watches, that I may meditate on Thy Word. Psalm 119:147, 148

I have rejoiced in the way of Thy testimonies, as much as in all riches. Psalm 119:114

The law of Thy mouth is better to me than thousands of gold and silver pieces. Psalm 119:72

Therefore I love Thy commandments above gold, yes, above fine gold Psalm 119:127

Here is a saint who would rather have God's Word than food, sleep, or money! Early in the morning and late at night he meditated on the Word of God and enriched his soul. It is this kind of a Christian who is able to use the Word of God to defeat Satan and his lies.

(4) *We must use God's Word.* The believer's mind should become like a "spiritual computer."

It should be so saturated with Scripture that when he faces a decision or a temptation, he automatically remembers the Scriptures that relate to that particular situation. It is the ministry of the Holy Spirit to bring God's Word to our minds when we need it.

> "But the Helper, the Holy Spirit, whom the Father will send in My name, He will teach you all things, and bring to your remembrance all that I said to you." John 14:26

But the Spirit of God cannot remind you of something *that you have not learned!* You must first let him teach you the Word. You must memorize the Scripture that he opens up to you. Then the Spirit of God will be able to remind you of what you have learned, and you can use that truth to battle Satan. Please keep in mind that Satan knows the Bible far better than we do! And he is able to quote it!

The Spirit of God will enable you to use the Word of God in the battle against the devil. The Spirit will show you when Satan is "using" the Bible to promote his own lies, as he did with Jesus in the wilderness. Satan quoted Psalm 91:11, 12, but he adapted it for his own purposes by omitting "in all your ways." God promises to protect us only when we are in his ways. If we foolishly go our own way, God is not obligated to care for us. This explains why Jesus replied, "On the other hand, it is written" (Matthew 4:7).

Jesus was comparing Scripture with Scripture. He was taking into consideration *the total mes-*

sage of the Bible and not stopping (as did Satan) with one isolated passage. Satan enjoys taking verses out of context and using them to "prove" his false claims. You and I must have a grasp of *all Scripture* if we are to detect Satan's lies and defeat them.

It is important, too, that we look at the world around us through the "eyes" of the Bible. We must

> *walk by faith, not by sight.* 2 Corinthians 5:7

If we try to evaluate things around us on the basis of our own thinking and knowledge, we will get into trouble. We must believe that what God says about things in his Word is true.

> *Therefore I esteem right all Thy precepts concerning everything, I hate every false way.* Psalm 119:128

A business proposition may "look right" to the natural mind, but if it is not based on the truths of God's Word, it will fail. A marriage may seem like "just the right thing" from the human perspective, but if it contradicts the Word of God, it is wrong. In my pastoral ministry, I have seen business deals fail and marriages collapse because they were not done according to the will of God. Somebody believed Satan's lie.

Taking Inventory
(1) Do I spend time daily reading God's Word and meditating on it?
(2) Do I systematically seek to memorize Scripture?

(3) Do I find myself automatically "thinking Bible" when I am tempted or when I face decisions, or must I telephone my Christian friends to get spiritual guidance?

(4) Do I find myself better able to detect Satan's lies?

(5) Are there any lies in my mind right now that I am believing?

(6) Do I know God's will for my life? Do I really *want* to know?

(7) Am I delighting in God's will and doing it from my heart?

(8) Am I guilty of telling lies? Why do I do it?

(9) Am I willing to take as true everything God's Word says about everything in my life? Or do I occasionally ask, "Has God *really* said that?" Do I argue with God's Word?

(10) Is the Word of God becoming more wonderful to me? Do I enjoy it more than the natural pleasures of life, including eating and sleeping?

A Suggestion. Ask your pastor to suggest a Bible memory program for you and your family. If he doesn't have one, then check your local Christian bookseller for such a program. You can also write to: The Navigators, P.O. Box 20, Colorado Springs, Colorado 80901.

TWO
The Destroyer

Be of sober spirit, be on the alert. Your adversary, the devil, prowls about like a roaring lion, seeking someone to devour. 1 Peter 5:8

"Simon, Simon, behold, Satan has demanded permission to sift you like wheat." Luke 22:31

They have as king over them, the angel of the abyss; his name in Hebrew is Abaddon [Destruction], and in the Greek he has the name Apollyon [Destroyer]. Revelation 9:11

Then there was brought to Him a demon-possessed man who was blind and dumb, and He healed him, so that the dumb man spoke and saw. Matthew 12:22

So the Lord said to Satan, "Behold, he [Job] is in your power, only spare his life." Job 2:6*

*I recommend you read the entire first two chapters of Job.

1. SATAN'S TARGET—YOUR BODY

If Satan cannot defeat you by deceiving your mind, he will then try to destroy your body. As the serpent, he deceives; as the lion, he devours. If we believe his lies, then we will destroy ourselves. As I write this chapter, authorities are investigating the mass suicide of members of the People's Temple in Guyana. Over 700 people died because they believed Satan's lies.

But if we resist his deceit, then he will attack our bodies. Job is the prime illustration of this kind of attack. He lost the fruit of his body—his children. He lost the means to sustain his body —his flocks and herds and wealth. And he lost the health of his body when he contracted a loathsome disease. His friends sat in silence for a week, for they saw that Job was in great agony. Even Job's wife was so overwhelmed by her husband's trials that she suggested, "Curse God and die!" (Job 2:9). Satan did a throrough job of attacking Job's body and all that related to it.

When you read the Gospel records you discover that Satan, through his demonic helpers, attacked and sought to destroy the bodies of various people. He caused one man to be dumb (Matthew 9:32, 33), and a woman to be bent over and disabled (Luke 13:11-17). He even attacked a child and tried to get him to destroy himself in the water or the fire (Matthew 17:14-18). There is no escaping the awesome fact that Satan wants to attack and destroy your body.

Why does he want to do this? For several reasons. To begin with, your body is *God's temple*.

Or do you not know that your body is a temple of the Holy Spirit who is in you, whom you have from God, and that you are not your own? For you have been bought with a price: therefore glorify God in your body. 1 Corinthians 6:19, 20

. . . according to my earnest expectation and hope, that I shall not be put to shame in anything, but that with all boldness, Christ shall even now, as always, be exalted in my body, whether by life or by death. Philippians 1:20

God is invisible; the world cannot see him. Jesus Christ has returned to heaven and cannot be seen. But we Christians *can* be seen, and it is our conduct *in the body* that glorifies and exalts the Lord.

Let your light shine before men in such a way that they may see your good works, and glorify your Father who is in heaven. Matthew 5:16

God wants to use your body as a vehicle for revealing him to a lost world. Unconverted people are not likely to read the Bible to learn about God, nor books of Christian theology; but they will read our lives.

But you are a chosen race, a royal priesthood, a holy nation, a people for God's own possession, that you may proclaim the excellencies of Him who has called you out of darkness into His marvelous light. 1 Peter 2:9

This means that when Satan attacks your body, he is attacking the one means God has of revealing his grace and love to a lost world. Creation reveals the power, wisdom, and glory of God; but Christians reveal the grace and love of God.

Not only is your body God's temple, but it is also *God's tool*.

> *Therefore do not let sin reign in your mortal body that you should obey its lusts, and do not go on presenting the members of your body to sin as instruments of unrighteousness; but present yourselves to God as those alive from the dead, and your members as instruments of righteousness to God.* Romans 6:12, 13

When God wanted an ark constructed, he used the skill of Noah and his family. When he wanted the tabernacle built, he used the hands and minds of Bezalel and Oholiab and their helpers (Exodus 36:1 ff.). Jesus used the hands of his disciples for the distributing of the bread and fish. He used their lips and tongues for the preaching of the gospel. If God is going to get his work done in this world, he must use the various members of our bodies, empowered by the Spirit of God.

Satan knows that he can hinder God's work by attacking God's workers and putting their "tools" out of commission. The Greek word translated "instruments" in Romans 6:13 can be translated "tool" or even "weapon." Just as God the Son had to take on a body to accomplish his work on earth, so the Holy Spirit needs our bodies. The members of your body are tools in the Spirit's hands to help build the Church here on earth. Never underestimate the importance of your body. Never minimize the care of your body. The Christian who is careless about his health or safety is playing right into the hands of the destroyer.

The third reason Satan attacks your body is because your body is *God's treasury*.

But we have this treasure in earthen vessels, that the surpassing greatness of the power may be of God and not from ourselves. 2 Corinthians 4:7

When God saved you, he put the treasure of eternal life within your body. You have the very life of God within you! God did not give you this great treasure simply to protect it—an earthen vessel is not the safest place for a treasure! He gave you this treasure that he might *invest it* through you in the lives of others. For example, God deposited this spiritual wealth in the Apostle Paul

according to the glorious gospel of the blessed God, with which I have been entrusted. 1 Timothy 1:11

Paul invested this treasure in Timothy.

O Timothy, guard what has been entrusted to you. 1 Timothy 6:20

> *Guard, through the Holy Spirit who dwells in us, the treasure which has been entrusted to you.* 2 Timothy 1:14

Timothy, in turn, was to invest this treasure in the lives of others.

> *And the things which you have heard from me in the presence of many witnesses, these entrust to faithful men, who will be able to teach others also.* 2 Timothy 2:2

In other words, the safety and success of this spiritual investment is in the hands of weak human beings! The treasure is in an earthen vessel! Satan can rob the world of spiritual wealth by attacking the bodies of believers.

Finally, Satan attacks your body because it is *God's testing-ground*.

> *But I buffet my body and make it my slave, lest possibly, after I have preached to others, I myself should be disqualified.* 1 Corinthians 9:27

The image here is that of the Greek games. Each participant had to qualify and keep the rules or he was not allowed to compete. If after he won a prize he was found guilty of breaking the rules, his prize was taken from him. Jim Thorpe, one of our greatest American athletes, had to return his Olympic medals because it was discovered he had earlier played sports for money, which is against Olympic rules.

Satan can rob you of your rewards by attacking your body and getting you to break the rules. It is not a matter of salvation, but of rewards for faithful service. The athlete did not lose his citizenship if he broke the rules; he only forfeited his reward, a shameful experience indeed.

> *And now, little children, abide in Him, so that when He appears, we may have confidence and not shrink away from Him in shame at His coming.* 1 John 2:28

I cannot emphasize too much that *your body is important to God.* As God's children, you and I must care for our bodies and use them for God's glory. Anything in our lives that keeps us from doing our best must be abandoned. Just as the mechanic takes good care of his tools, so the believer takes good care of the "tools" of his body.

> *I urge you therefore, brethren, by the mercies of God, to present your bodies a living and holy sacrifice, acceptable to God, which is your spiritual service of worship.* Romans 12:1

2. SATAN'S WEAPON—SUFFERING

Satan wants to control the circumstances around the body so that the believer will suffer. He wants to touch the body and create suffering. All of this is illustrated in the story of Job. First, Satan attacked Job's *body* through the circumstances around him, and Job lost his children, his wealth, and the favor of his wife, friends, and neighbors. Then Satan attacked Job's *person* with a horrible disease. When Job looked around, his situation was painful. When he looked within, it was even more painful. And when he looked up, it seemed that God had forsaken him, although Job maintained his faith in God and was honored at the end.

It is important to note that *God was always in control.* Satan could not attack Job's possessions until God gave him permission. Satan could not attack Job's person until God allowed it. This reminds us of our Lord's words to Peter.

> *"Simon, Simon, behold, Satan has demanded permission* [literally "obtained by asking"] *to sift you like wheat; but I have prayed for you, that your faith may not fail."* Luke 22:31, 32

Satan cannot touch the child of God without the heavenly Father's permission. This is a great encouragement to us, for we know that whatever suffering may come to our lives, God has ordained it and is in complete control. The one thing God will not control is *how we respond to this suffering,* and it is here that Satan can gain his purpose.

Note, too, that there is more than one kind of suffering in the life of the Christian. There is *natural suffering* that we experience simply because we are human. We cannot prevent the gradual breakdown of the body as we grow old, though we can seek to delay it. We are subject to sickness and injury; we lose loved ones and friends as death claims them; we find ourselves slowing down when we wish we could speed things up. The inconvenience, and even the pain, of being a weak human being in a dangerous world cannot be blamed on the devil. All of creation is groaning because of the bondage of sin, and we Christians are groaning with it (Romans 8:18-23).

God sometimes sends (or permits) his children to suffer that he might discipline them. Our heavenly Father loves us too much to permit us to be rebels, so he chastens us that we might conform to his will.

> My son, do not regard lightly the discipline of the Lord, nor faint when you are reproved by Him; for those whom the Lord loves He disciplines, and He scourges every son whom He receives. Hebrews 12:5, 6

The word translated "discipline" in Hebrews 12 simply means "child-training." The purpose of discipline is the maturity of the son. God's purpose is not to persecute us, but to perfect us. Chastening is not the work of an angry judge as he punishes a criminal. It is the work of a loving Father as he perfects a child.

This chastening is not always because we have sinned. True, God does "spank" his children if they rebel and refuse to repent. David sinned against God and tried to hide his sin for a year or more. Read Psalm 32 and discover what David suffered physically, emotionally, and spiritually because he would not submit to God. But sometimes God permits suffering in our lives simply to build us up and help us mature.

Two storms in the Bible illustrate this truth.

Jonah disobeyed God and refused to go to Nineveh. He found a convenient ship to take him to Tarshish, but God interrupted Jonah's escape by sending a storm. When the mariners threw Jonah into the stormy sea, the prophet was swallowed by a great fish. He describes his "living death" in the stomach of the great fish in Chapter 2 of his book. God had to chasten Jonah and almost take his life before the prophet would confess his sins and surrender to God. This storm came for the purpose of *correcting* God's servant who had been disobedient.

But there are storms that come *because we are obedient!* One such storm is recorded in Matthew 14:22-33. Jesus had fed more than 5,000 people and they wanted to make him king. He sent the crowd away, and also sent the disciples across the Sea of Galilee in their boat. He went up to the mountaintop to pray. When the disciples got away from the land, a fierce storm arose and almost sank the ship. Please note: they were not in the storm because they disobeyed the Lord, *but because they obeyed him.* He was testing and perfecting their faith. Later he came to them and stilled the storm; but the entire experience revealed to the men how weak their faith really was.

So, we sometimes suffer simply because we are human. We suffer, too, because we disobey the Lord and need to be chastened. We also suffer that God might perfect our faith and help us mature. Not all suffering is Satanic in origin. But there is a kind of suffering that is Satan's weapon, and that is what Job experienced. It seemed that all of the calamities in his life had perfectly natural explanations: the Sabeans took the oxen and donkeys; fire from heaven (perhaps lightning) burned the sheep; the Chaldeans took the camels; and a great wind (a tornado?) wrecked his oldest son's house and killed all of Job's children. *But Satan was behind all of them!* When God gives him permission, Satan can use people and the forces of nature to accomplish his purposes.

As believers, we have this confidence: *God is always in complete control.* When God permits Satan to light the furnace, he always keeps his own hand on the thermostat! Job did not know what was going on behind the scenes. He had no idea that God was permitting him to suffer so that Satan might be silenced. The real battle was "in the heavenly places" (Ephesians 6:12). Job's home and body were only the arena in which the two combatants—God and Satan—were struggling against each other. Satan wanted to use Job's body to defeat God, and God wanted to use Job's body to defeat Satan.

When you find yourself in difficult circumstances, seek to discern through the Word and prayer whether your suffering is from nature, from God, or from Satan. Is God perfecting you? Is he disciplining you? Is Satan seeking to hinder your ministry or even destroy you? You cannot control the *origin* of your suffering, but you can control the *outcome*. How? This leads us to our next section.

3. SATAN'S PURPOSE—
TO MAKE YOU IMPATIENT WITH GOD'S WILL

The only place in the New Testament where Job is named is James 5:11:

> *Behold, we count those blessed who endured. You have heard of the endurance of Job and have seen the outcome of the Lord's dealings, that the Lord is full of compassion and is merciful.*

This verse indicates that Satan's purpose was to try to get Job to be impatient and give up. Job did become impatient with himself and his critical friends, but he never lost his faith in God. Though he did not understand what God was doing, Job knew that he could trust God and that God would vindicate him in the end.

Patience is an important Christian virtue. Unless we have patience, we can never learn many of the truths that God wants us to learn, truths that will lead us into a deeper life and a more fruitful ministry.

> *Consider it all joy, my brethren, when you encounter various trials, knowing that the testing of your faith produces endurance. And let endurance have its perfect result, that you may be perfect and complete, lacking in nothing. James 1:2-4*

Children are usually impatient; they cannot sit still long enough to get the things done that need to be done. "How long do we have to wait?" is the stock question of the child. *Impatience is a mark of immaturity.*

But impatience is also *a mark of unbelief.* "He who believes will not be in a hurry" (Isaiah 28:16, literal translation). When you find yourself restless and nervous, anxious to "do something," you can be sure you are not trusting God to work. You and I need to be

> *imitators of those who through* faith *and* patience *inherit the promises.* Hebrews 6:12

Faith and patience go together. If we really trust God, then we will wait on him to accomplish what he has promised.

Impatience is not only a mark of immaturity and unbelief, but it is *a mark of fleshly living.* The flesh (the old nature) is always impatient, but the fruit of the Spirit is

> *love, joy, peace,* patience, *kindness, goodness, faithfulness, gentleness, self-control.* Galatians 5:22, 23

By nature, we are impatient; but the new nature within can produce patience as we yield to the Holy Spirit. Whenever you find an impulsive, impatient believer, you can be reasonably sure that that person is not walking in the Spirit, but is living by the energy of the flesh.

Impatience always leads to costly mistakes. Abraham became impatient with God and "married" Hagar, his wife's handmaid, in order to bring a son into the world and fulfill God's promise. A son was born, but he caused nothing but trouble! Abraham had to wait another fourteen years for Isaac to be born, and Isaac brought joy and blessing to the home.

King Saul became impatient and would not wait for the prophet Samuel to come. He rushed ahead of God's will and offered the sacrifice, and this was the beginning of the end of his kingdom.

Peter became impatient in the Garden of Gethsemane and tried to kill a man with his sword! Instead of cutting the man's throat, Peter only severed his ear; and Jesus, to save Peter's life, healed the wound. Peter's impatience almost cost him his life.

Satan knows that if he can make us impatient, he can lead us to do something stupid and get ourselves and others into trouble. I recall a friend who became impatient in his ministry, hastily resigned from the church, and accepted a church that was supposed to be "heaven on earth." It turned out to be just the opposite, and within a year my friend was moving again. I remember another friend who thought he found a "get rich quick" job, jumped into it, and almost lost everything he had. Fortunately his old boss took him back, but my friend had to start on a lower rung of the ladder. Impatience is costly.

But patient endurance is enriching. Satan tempts us that he might bring out the worst in us, but God permits it that he might bring out the best in us. Job knew this; therefore, he said:

But He knows the way I take; when He has tried me, I shall come forth as gold. Job 23:10

God will never permit the enemy to put us through the fire without his having a definite purpose in mind. *God wants to make you patient.* We cannot learn patience by reading a book or hearing a lecture. The only way we can learn patience is by *going through the trials that God assigns to us.* The trials of life are the tools God uses to mature us, to build our faith, and to get us to trust the Spirit and not the flesh.

When you find yourself impatient, you can be sure that Satan and the flesh are at work, and that you are in danger of making a wrong decision. When the circumstances of life are irritating, that is the time to beware! When family problems, friends, finances, or feelings are making life uncomfortable, then you can be sure Satan is near, waiting for an opportunity to attack.

But God has given you a defense!

4. YOUR DEFENSE—
THE IMPARTED GRACE OF GOD

Job is not the only saint who felt Satan's attack against his body, for the great Apostle Paul had a similar experience.

And because of the surpassing greatness of the revelations, for this reason, to keep me from exalting myself, there was given me a thorn in the flesh, a messenger of Satan to buffet me—to keep me from exalting myself! Concerning this I entreated the Lord three times that it might depart from me. And He has said to me, "My grace is sufficient for you, for power is perfected in weakness." Most gladly, therefore, I will rather boast about my weaknesses, that the power of Christ may dwell in me. Therefore I am well content with weaknesses, with insults, with distresses, with persecutions, with difficulties, for Christ's sake; for when I am weak, then I am strong. 2 Corinthians 12:7-10

We do not know what Paul's "thorn in the flesh" was; but whatever it was, it buffeted him enough to make him pray three times for healing. (You will recall that our Lord prayed three times in the Garden that the cup might pass from him. When difficulties come, it is not wrong to pray for deliverance.) God did not answer Paul's prayer, *but God did meet Paul's need.* "My grace is sufficient for you." It is the imparted grace of God that gives us victory when Satan attacks the body with suffering. Only by the grace of God can we have the patient endurance that we need as we go through the furnace.

And after you have suffered for a little while, the God of all grace, who called you to His eternal glory in Christ, will himself perfect, confirm, strengthen and establish you. 1 Peter 5:10

Our God is "the God of all grace." The Holy Spirit who indwells us is "the Spirit of grace" (Hebrews 10:29). God's throne is a "throne of grace" (Hebrews 4:16), and his Word is "the word of His grace" (Acts 20:32). It is grace from start to finish!

God's grace is God's provision for our every need. Grace is not a "mystical substance" that God pours into us when we have a need. Grace is God's bountiful supply of our every need.

"Law" means that I must do something for God, but "grace" means that God does something for me. Grace cannot be deserved. Grace cannot be earned. *Grace can only be given.*

To begin with, you were *saved by God's grace.*

For by grace you have been saved through faith; and that not of yourselves, it is the gift of God; not as a result of works, that no one should boast. Ephesians 2:8, 9

This means that "the riches of His grace" are now available to you (Ephesians 2:7). God can give you grace for *serving* (1 Corinthians 15:9, 10), for *sacrificing* (2 Corinthians 8:1-9), for *singing* (Colossians 3:16, margin), and even for *speaking* (Colossians 4:6). It also means that God can give you grace for *suffering*, as he did with Job and Paul.

What steps, then, should you take when Satan attacks your body with suffering and tries to make you impatient with God's will?

(1) *Immediately submit yourself to God.* If you rebel, you will give Satan another foothold in your life. Tell God exactly how you feel, but also tell him that you love him and will trust him, come what may.

Though He slay me, I will hope in Him. Job 13:15

(2) *Thank God for the trials.*

Always giving thanks for all things in the name of our Lord Jesus Christ to God, even the Father. Ephesians 5:20

In everything give thanks; for this is God's will for you in Christ Jesus. 1 Thessalonians 5:18

This does not mean you *enjoy* the suffering, but only that you rejoice because you are suffering in the will of God and you know that he is in control. Satan hates it when believers thank God in their trials. When Paul and Silas sang and praised God in that Philippian jail, they completely ruined all of Satan's plans! (Read Acts 16:14 ff.)

(3) *Spend much time in the Word of God.* It is the "word of His grace" (Acts 20:32), and the gracious promises of God will strengthen you. Remember: we do not live on explanations; we live on promises. God did not explain to Abraham everything that he was doing, but he did give Abraham all the promises he needed to keep going.

Before I was afflicted I went astray, but now I keep Thy word. . . . It is good for me that I was afflicted, that I may learn Thy statutes. Psalm 119:67, 71

You will discover in God's Word the promises and encouragements that you need for each day.

For whatever was written in earlier times was written for our instruction, that through perseverance and the encouragement of the Scriptures *we might have hope.* Romans 15:4

(4) *Look for ways to glorify Christ.* Remember, God wants to use your body to glorify him; Satan wants to use your body to disgrace the

Lord. Patience in suffering always glorifies God. Unconverted people cannot understand how Christians can suffer and not complain or rebel.

> For what credit is there if, when you sin and are harshly treated, you endure it with patience? But if when you do what is right and suffer for it you patiently endure it, this finds favor with God. 1 Peter 2:20

> But if anyone suffers as a Christian, let him not feel ashamed, but in that name let him glorify God. 1 Peter 4:16

In the midst of shame and suffering, Paul and Silas glorified God by singing and praising his name. While he was being stoned to death, Stephen glorified God by praying for his murderers. Many of David's psalms record the fact that he could praise God even when persecuted and rejected. Paul's most joyful letter—Philippians —was written from Roman imprisonment when his life was in the balance.

As you follow these instructions, you will discover the Spirit of grace working in your life and imparting to you the grace of God. You will grow in patient endurance! You will experience God's love and grace within, and this experience will more than compensate for the inconvenience and suffering without. God may not change the circumstances, *but he will change you* so that the circumstances will work *for you* and not *against you.* As I said before, you and I cannot control the *origin* or the *operation* of suffering, but we can (with God's help) control the *outcome.*

Most gladly, therefore, I will rather boast about my weaknesses, that the power of Christ may dwell in me. 2 Corinthians 12:9

If you live to please yourself, then Satan will win. If you live to glorify God, Satan will lose. The imparted grace of God is the only weapon that can defeat him, and that grace can be found only in "the God of all grace."

THREE
The Ruler

"Now is judgment upon this world; now the ruler of this world shall be cast out." John 12:31

"I will not speak much more with you, for the ruler of the world is coming, and he has nothing in Me." John 14:30

... and not a new convert, lest he become conceited and fall into the condemnation incurred by the devil. And he must have a good reputation with those outside the church, so that he may not fall into reproach and the snare of the devil. 1 Timothy 3:6, 7

Pride goes before destruction, and a haughty spirit before stumbling. Proverbs 16:18

We know that we are of God, and the whole world lies in the power of [literally *"in the lap of"*] *the evil one.* 1 John 5:19

If I were to ask you, "What was David's great sin?" you would probably reply, "Committing adultery with Bathsheba and then having her husband killed in battle." Certainly the sins of adultery and murder (coupled with deceit) are great sins and must not be treated lightly. But David committed another sin that had even greater consequences. Because of David's adultery, four persons died: Uriah, the baby that was born, Amnon, and Absalom. But because of David's other sin, *70,000 people died!* When David confessed his sins of adultery and murder, he said, "I have sinned." But when he confessed this other sin, he said, "I have sinned greatly."

What was David's other sin? And what part did Satan play in it?

> Then Satan stood up against Israel and moved David to number Israel. So David said to Joab and to the princes of the people, "Go, number Israel from Beer-sheba even to Dan, and bring me word that I may know their number."
>
> And God was displeased with this thing, so He struck Israel. And David said to God, "I have sinned greatly, in that I have done this thing. But now, please take away the iniquity of Thy servant, for I have done very foolishly."
>
> The Lord sent a pestilence on Israel; 70,000 men of Israel fell. And God sent an angel to Jerusalem to destroy it; but as he was about to destroy it, the Lord saw and was sorry over the calamity, and said to the destroying angel, "It is enough; now relax your hand." And the angel of the Lord was standing by the threshing floor of Ornan the Jebusite.
>
> Then David lifted up his eyes and saw the angel of the Lord standing between earth and

heaven, with his drawn sword in his hand
stretched out over Jerusalem. Then David
and the elders, covered with sackcloth, fell
on their faces. And David said to God, "Is it
not I who commanded to count the people?
Indeed, I am the one who has sinned and
done very wickedly, but these sheep, what
have they done? O Lord my God, please let
Thy hand be against me and my father's
household, but not against Thy people that
they should be plagued."

Then the angel of the Lord commanded
Gad to say to David, that David should go
up and build an altar to the Lord on the
threshing floor of Ornan the Jebusite. So
David went up at the word of Gad, which he
spoke in the name of the Lord. 1 Chronicles
21:1, 2, 7, 8, 14-19.

1. SATAN'S TARGET—YOUR WILL

Satan's goal is always to get to the will and control it. He may begin by deceiving the mind, as
with Eve, or by attacking the body, as with Job;
but ultimately he must get to the will. However,
in David's case, Satan bypassed the mind and the
body and in a blitzkrieg action attacked his will
and won. David's mind was not deceived; he had
his eyes wide open when he rebelled against God.
David was not suffering; in fact, his kingdom
was in great shape. He had won a number of
notable victories and was enjoying a height of
popularity and success. Had David been de-

ceived, or had he been suffering, we might have had reason to sympathize with his decision; but this was not the case.

We must never underestimate the importance of the will in the Christian life. Too many believers have an *intellectual* religion that satisfies the mind but never changes the life. They can discuss the Bible and even argue about it; but when it comes to living it, they fail. Other Christians have an *emotional* religion that is made up of changing feelings. Unless they are on an emotional high, they feel God has forsaken them. God wants *the whole of the inner man* to be devoted to him: an intelligent mind, a fervent heart, and an obedient will. Our obedience ought to be intelligent, and it ought to be motivated from a warm and loving heart.

The Christian life is basically a matter of the will. We are to love the Lord with all our heart (the emotions) and our mind (the intellect) and our strength (the will). The Holy Spirit wants to instruct the mind through the Word, inspire the heart with true holy emotions, and then strengthen the will to do the will of God. A dedicated Christian prays whether he feels like it or not. He obeys the Word of God regardless of his own feelings. The believer who lives on his emotions is repeatedly up and down; he lives on a religious roller coaster. But the believer who lives on the basis of "spiritual willpower" has a consistent Christian life and a steady ministry that is not threatened by changing circumstances or feelings.

guilty of sins of the spirit: pride, stubbornness (which is passed off as "conviction"), gossip, jealousy, competition, bragging about results, etc.

To some degree, pride enters into all of Satan's temptations. "You shall be as God!" was part of his offer to Eve. Job had to listen to the criticisms of his friends, and he wondered why God did not appear to vindicate him. When Satan tempted our Lord, he tried to appeal to human pride.

> *Again, the devil took Him to a very high mountain, and showed Him all the kingdoms of the world, and their glory; and he said to Him, "All these things will I give You, if You fall down and worship me."* Matthew 4:8, 9

This is one of the dangers of great success. Those to whom much is given fight intensive spiritual battles against pride. Pride glorifies man and robs God of the glory that only he deserves. Pride is a weapon that Satan wields with great skill. This explains why Peter writes,

> *God is opposed to the proud, but gives grace to the humble. Humble yourselves, therefore, under the mighty hand of God, that He may exalt you at the proper time.* 1 Peter 5:5, 6

What was so wrong about David numbering the people? After all, in Exodus 30:11-16 didn't Moses *command* an annual census? Yes, he did, *as a reminder to the nation that it had been purchased by God.* Each male twenty years of age or older had to give half a shekel for "ransom money." It was his way of acknowledging God's great redemption from Egypt. Note in verse 12 that Moses added a warning: " . . . that there may be no plague among them when you number them."

When David numbered the people, he did it for his own glory and not for the glory of God. There is no record that the "redemption money" was collected. It was "the king's word" and not the Word of God that directed the census; and even Joab (who was hardly a spiritual man) resisted the king's commandment. It was pride that motivated David's actions. Satan got hold of David's will, inflated David's ego, and led him into sin. Satan knew that David was feeling victorious and important, and he took advantage of the situation.

This explains why Paul admonished the early church not to put new Christians into places of spiritual leadership.

> *And not a new convert, lest he become conceited and fall into the condemnation incurred by the devil.* 1 Timothy 3:6

In my years of pastoral ministry I have seen young Christians thrust into places of ministry for which they were not prepared, and the consequences have been painful. Satan whispers to the new Christian who is given a place of leadership, "Now you are somebody important!" It is not long before his pride takes over and he becomes a problem to the pastor and the church. The Apostle John had this kind of problem with church leaders in his day.

> *I wrote something to the church; but Diotrephes, who loves to be first among them, does not accept what we say.* 3 John 9

Imagine! refusing to accept the words of an apostle! Paul had something to say about this attitude:

> *If any one advocates a different doctrine, and does not agree with sound words, those of our Lord Jesus Christ, and with the doctrine conforming to godliness, he is conceited and understands nothing; but he has a morbid interest in controversial questions and disputes about words, out of which arise envy, strife, abusive language, evil suspicions, and constant friction between men of depraved mind and deprived of the truth.*
> 1 Timothy 6:3-5

Satan's desire is to work *in* the local church, to hinder its ministry; and to do this, he must work in and through Christians or professed Christians who are a part of that fellowship. Pride is one of his chief weapons. If he can get a pastor proud of his preaching, a Sunday school teacher proud of his class's growth, or a church officer proud of his experience and leadership, then Satan has a foothold from which to launch his attack. King David brought death and sorrow to Israel simply because he was proud.

3. SATAN'S PURPOSE— TO MAKE YOU INDEPENDENT OF GOD'S WILL

Man is a dependent creature. He must depend on God ("for in Him we live and move and exist,"

Acts 17:28) and on his fellowman in order to stay alive. The essence of sin is to seek to be independent of God. It is to make ourselves the Creator instead of the creatures (Romans 1:25). It is to believe Satan's lie, "You will be like God." If Satan can get you to act and think independently of God's will, he can then control your will and control your life. You will think that you are acting freely, which is part of Satan's deception; but actually you will be acting under orders from the ruler of this world.

As we have learned in previous chapters, the will of God is the most important thing in the believer's life. As the deceiver, Satan seeks to make you ignorant of God's will. As the destroyer, he seeks to make you impatient with God's will. In both cases, the will of God will not be at work in your life. But even if Satan does not deceive your mind and make you ignorant, or attack your body and make you impatient, he will try to control your will through pride so that you will think and act independently of the holy will of God.

I recall a young lady who consulted me about her wedding. I was her pastor, and I had cautioned her against marrying an unbeliever. The young man she was dating was not a Christian; in fact, he was not even much of a gentleman. I had pointed out to her verses such as 2 Corinthians 6:14-18 and 1 Corinthians 7:39, but she was not interested. Finally she shouted to me as she left my office, "I don't care what you say. I don't care what the Bible says. I'm going to marry him!" And she did, and the last I heard she was not in fellowship with the church or serving the Lord. She acted independently of God's will.

Whenever you and I act in direct disobedience to the will of God, we are displaying pride and independence. It may not be in a great matter such as marriage; it might be in connection with something we think is trivial and unimportant. *But everything in our lives is important to God.* There are in his Word precepts, principles, and promises that guide us as we seek to know his will. Of course, this does not mean that we should become fanatical about the matter and quit making our own decisions on the basis of common sense and the Spirit's direction. I recall a fellow seminary student who almost lost his mind because he prayed about what breakfast food to eat, what corner to cross at, and what book to study next. There may be situations in our lives when praying about such matters would be vitally important, but not usually. As we walk with the Lord, we learn to discern his will in matters that are not too consequential.

God gave David nearly ten months in which to repent and call off the census, but he persisted in his stubborn way. This subtle sin of pride keeps feeding itself and getting stronger. David was not guilty of "the lust of the eyes" (as when he looked at Bathsheba), or "the lust of the flesh" (as when he committed adultery with her); but he was guilty of "the pride of life" (see 1 John 2:15-17). Pride means that we act independently of God, or worse yet that we try to *use God* to accomplish our own selfish purposes. God becomes our heavenly slave and we tell him what he must do!

A man phoned me long-distance to share his problem. He had heard me over the radio and thought perhaps I could help him. He had pulled a shady deal on the stock market, had lost a bundle of money, and wanted to know how to get out of the mess he was in. The only thing I could suggest was that he confess his sin to the Lord and to anybody else who was involved, and ask God to give him the grace he would need to start over again. He had acted independently of God's will, ignored the Bible's warnings against deceit and stealing, and now had to suffer the painful consequences. When we rebel against God and go it alone, we cannot expect him to run in and rescue us. God in his grace does forgive our sins; but God in his government must permit sin to run its course and produce its natural results. There is no way to escape the fact that we reap what we sow.

David knew this, and that explains why he did not try to sneak out of the mess he had created. Seventy thousand Israelites died! God's hand of judgment was against his people! The higher a person is in spiritual position, the more his sins will affect others. David's adultery affected his family and, to some degree, the nation; but his numbering of the people created a national crisis.

One of the most important lessons the believer must learn is that he cannot be independent of God. He needs God's provisions to sustain him physically, and he needs God's will and God's Word to sustain him spiritually. Success, the praise of men, and even the blessing of God can so inflate the ego that we think we can get along without God. Speaking of King Uzziah, the Bible says,

> Hence his fame spread afar, for he was marvelously helped until he was strong. But when he became strong, his heart was so proud that he acted corruptly, and he was unfaithful to the Lord his God. 2 Chronicles 26:15, 16

Moses gave this same warning to the people of Israel.

> "Then it shall come about when the Lord your God brings you into the land which He swore to your fathers . . . then watch yourself, lest you forget the Lord who brought you from the land of Egypt, out of the house of slavery." Deuteronomy 6:10, 12

No wonder the Apostle Paul was glad for his thorn in the flesh.

> For when I am weak, then I am strong. 2 Corinthians 12:10

Beware when you feel you have arrived! Beware when you feel you are very important and that God could not get along without you! Beware when you start to rob God of the glory that belongs only to him!

What is your defense?

4. YOUR DEFENSE—
THE INDWELLING SPIRIT OF GOD

Pride is such a strong weapon, and Satan is such a strong adversary, that only a stronger power can give us victory. That power comes from the Holy Spirit of God.

> So then, my beloved, just as you have always obeyed, not as in my presence only, but now much more in my absence, work out your own salvation with fear and trembling; for it is God who is at work in you, both to will and to work for His good pleasure. Philippians 2:12, 13

Only God the Holy Spirit, working in you, can control your will and enable you to please God.

"Work out your own salvation" does not mean "work for your own salvation." Salvation is a free gift, purchased by the blood of Jesus Christ. To "work out your own salvation" means to bring your Christian life to completion, to accomplish in character and conduct what God has planned for you. The Greek word means "to carry out to the goal, to bring to the ultimate conclusion." God has a definite plan for each life, and we must cooperate with him in fulfilling that plan. According to Ephesians 2:8-10, there are three "works" involved in the Christian life:

> For by grace you have been saved through faith; and that not of yourselves, it is the gift of God; not as a result of works, that no one should boast. For we are His workmanship, created in Christ Jesus for good works, which

God prepared beforehand, that we should walk in them.

The first work that Paul names is *salvation* —the work that God does *for* you. This work was completed by Jesus Christ on the cross.

"I have glorified Thee on the earth, having accomplished the work which Thou hast given Me to do." John 17:4

When Jesus therefore had received the sour wine, He said, "It is finished!" And He bowed His head, and gave up His spirit. John 19:30

But He, having offered one sacrifice for sins for all time, sat down at the right hand of God. Hebrews 10:12

Everything else that God does in your life is based on this finished work of Christ.

The second work is *sanctification* —the work that God does *in* you. Salvation is but the beginning; it must be followed by spiritual growth and development.

But grow in the grace and knowledge of our Lord and Savior Jesus Christ. 2 Peter 3:18

This leads to the third work—*service*, the work that God does *through* you. God works *in* you that he might work *through* you and accomplish the tasks that he has already prepared *for* you. It is not necessary for us to manufacture things to do for God; he already has a perfect plan for our lives and special works that he wants us to fulfill for his glory.

How does God work *in* us? Through his Holy Spirit. But what must we do to enable the Spirit of God to work in us? The answer to that question is found in two of the most familiar verses in the Bible—Romans 12:1, 2:

> *I urge you therefore, brethren, by the mercies of God, to present* your bodies *a living and holy sacrifice, acceptable to God, which is your spiritual service of worship. And do not be conformed to this world, but be transformed by the renewing of* your mind, *that you may prove what* the will of God *is, that which is good and acceptable and perfect.*

The Holy Spirit can work in your life when your body, mind, and will are yielded to him.

But these are the very areas which Satan wants to attack! He wants to attack your *body* with suffering to make you impatient with God's will. He wants to attack your *mind* with lies to make you ignorant of God's will. And he wants to attack your *will* with pride to make you independent of God's will.

If you yield these three areas of your life *daily* to the Spirit of God, then the Spirit will empower you to defeat the devil. As the Spirit of grace, he will give grace to your body so that you will be able to endure suffering to the glory of God. As the Spirit of wisdom, he will teach you God's Word and bring it to your mind when Satan attacks with his lies. And as the Spirit of power, he will empower your will to say "No!" to pride. The Holy Spirit will work in you and through you to defeat the wicked one.

74

Remember: in the battle against Satan, the only way to conquer is to surrender—surrender to God.

Therefore it says, "God is opposed to the proud, but gives grace to the humble." Submit therefore *to God.* Resist the devil *and he will flee from you.* James 4:7

Let me be very practical about this matter of Christian surrender. The verb "present" in Romans 12:1 carries the meaning of "a once-for-all surrender." It is not necessary for you to keep walking an aisle to be a yielded believer. Make a once-for-all presentation to God of your body, mind, and will. But it is good to reaffirm that surrender at the beginning of each day. When you first awaken, immediately give your body to God as an act of faith; and prove that you mean it *by getting out of bed.* The discipline of getting up in the morning is a part of spiritual victory.

The next step is to reach for your Bible and present your mind to God for spiritual renewal. It is the Word of God that renews the mind and transforms it. If you do not have a system for reading the Bible, get one. Personally, I like to read straight through the Bible regularly, but I do not give myself a time limit. I start in Genesis 1, Psalm 1, and Matthew 1, and I keep reading. There are some days when I read and meditate on only a few verses; on other days, I may read all three chapters. I am not in a hurry; I am not trying to set any records. My purpose is to meditate on the Word of God so that the Spirit of God will be able to transform my mind and make it more spiritual.

After you have given God your body (and gotten out of bed) and your mind (and meditated on the Word), your next step is to give him your will; and this you do in prayer. The Word of God and prayer always go together.

"But we will devote ourselves to prayer, and to the ministry of the word." Acts 6:4

"If you abide in Me, and My words abide in you, ask whatever you wish, and it shall be done for you." John 15:7

If you have only the Word, without prayer, you will have light without heat; but if you have prayer without the Word, you will be in danger of becoming a fanatic—heat without light or "zeal . . . not in accordance with knowledge" (Rom. 10:2). The important thing in prayer is to yield your will to God's will in the matters that you pray about.

When you have taken these three steps, you will have surrendered yourself totally to the Lord —body, mind, and will. The Spirit of God will be able to work in you and give you victory. The Holy Spirit uses the Word.

And for this reason we also constantly thank God that when you received from us the word of God's message, you accepted it not as the word of men, but for what it really is, the word of God, which also performs its work in you who believe. 1 Thessalonians 2:13

Now to Him who is able to do exceeding abundantly beyond all that we ask or think, according to the power that works within us . . . Ephesians 3:20

When God's Spirit is at work in us, he produces *humility* and not pride. Humility is not thinking meanly of yourself ("I'm not worth anything! I can't do anything!"); humility is simply not thinking of yourself at all! The Christian must be honest with himself and with God. That is why Romans 12:3 is in the Bible.

> *For through the grace given to me I say to every man among you not to think more highly of himself than he ought to think; but to think so as to have sound judgment, as God has allotted to each a measure of faith.*

When God called Moses to go to Egypt to deliver Israel, Moses argued with God. He protested that he was slow of speech and could not do the job. Was this humility on Moses' part? Of course not! It was pride; in fact, it was the worse kind of pride: false humility. The person who is truly humble has these characteristics: (1) he knows himself; (2) he accepts himself; (3) he yields himself to God; (4) he seeks to better himself that he might serve God better. The humble man realizes that all that he has comes from God and must be given back to God. John the Baptist said:

> *"A man can receive nothing, unless it have been given him from heaven."* John 3:27

And Paul echoed this truth:

> *For who regards you as superior? And what do you have that you did not receive? But if*

77

you did receive it, why do you boast as if you had not received it! 1 Corinthians 4:7

To boast of your gifts is a sin, because God gave them to you and you cannot take credit for them. But to *deny* your gifts is also a sin. We must accept our gifts and affirm our gifts to the glory of God. We must not think more highly of ourselves than we ought, but neither should we think *less* of ourselves!

So when Satan comes with pride to attack your will, surrender immediately to the Holy Spirit and let him work in you to produce humility and submission before God. Do not attempt to go beyond your gifts or the faith you have to exercise those gifts. Satan can use *spiritual* things to make you proud: your ability to teach or preach the Word; your prayer life; your success in witnessing and soul-winning.

The story may be apocryphal, but it illustrates the point. A famous Christian businessman was visiting a church and was asked to give a word of greeting. He got carried away telling all that God had done for him. "I have a successful business, a large house, a lovely family, a famous name, enough money to do the things I want to do and be able to give to Christian works. I have health and opportunities unnumbered. There are many people who would gladly exchange places with me. What more could God give me?" From the back of the auditorium a voice called, "A good dose of humility!"

Humble yourselves in the presence of the Lord, and He will exalt you. James 4:10

FOUR
The Accuser

And I heard a loud voice in heaven, saying, "Now the salvation, and the power, and the kingdom of our God and the authority of His Christ have come, for the accuser of our brethren has been thrown down, who accuses them before our God day and night."
Revelation 12:10

But whom you forgive anything, I forgive also . . . in order that no advantage be taken of us by Satan; for we are not ignorant of his schemes. 2 Corinthians 2:10, 11

For the sorrow that is according to the will of God produces a repentance without regret, leading to salvation; but the sorrow of the world produces death. 2 Corinthians 7:10

Suppose that the believer does not take advantage of his victorious position in Christ.

Suppose he refuses to use the spiritual defenses provided. *Suppose the believer sins.* What then?

You would think that Satan, having led the person into sin, would then leave him to suffer the consequences; but this is not what happens. Satan has one more strategem that can make the disobedient Christian *doubly defeated.* We read about it in Zechariah 3.

> Then he showed me Joshua the high priest standing before the angel of the Lord, and Satan standing at his right hand to accuse him. And the Lord said to Satan, "The Lord rebuke you, Satan! Indeed, the Lord who has chosen Jerusalem rebuke you! Is this not a brand plucked from the fire?"
>
> Now Joshua was clothed with filthy garments and standing before the angel. And he spoke and said to those who were standing before him saying, "Remove the filthy garments from him." Again he said to him, "See, I have taken your iniquity away from you and will clothe you with festal robes." Then I said, "Let them put a clean turban on his head." So they put a clean turban on his head and clothed him with garments, while the angel of the Lord was standing by.
>
> And the angel of the Lord admonished Joshua saying, "Thus says the Lord of hosts, 'If you will walk in My ways, and if you will perform My service, then you will also govern My house and also have charge of My courts, and I will grant you free access among these who are standing here.'"

1. SATAN'S TARGET—
YOUR HEART AND CONSCIENCE

This scene, unlike the other three we have examined, is in heaven. The setting is that of a courtroom: God is the Judge, Joshua the high priest is the defendant, and Satan is the prosecutor trying to prove Joshua guilty. Satan appears to have a case, because Joshua is wearing filthy garments and the high priest was always to wear clean clothes. The prophet Zechariah had this vision at a time when the nation of Israel had sinned against the Lord. The people had returned to Palestine after their Babylonian captivity, and there was hope that the nation would obey God and serve him. But sad to say, they had not learned their lesson. When you read the books of Ezra and Nehemiah, and the prophecies of Zechariah, Haggai, and Malachi, you discover that the Jewish men were divorcing their wives and marrying heathen women; that Jewish merchants were charging their brethren exorbitant interest rates; and that even the priests were robbing God and keeping the best of the sacrifices for themselves.

This explains why Joshua's priestly garments were dirty. He represented the people before God, and the people were sinful. Satan knew that they were sinful, and he protested to God that Israel should be judged. You can imagine Satan's arguments:

"Have you considered your servants in Israel, that they are a rebellious and disobedient people? You chastened them in Babylon, hoping to teach them obedience. Now they have returned to their land by your goodness—and they are disobeying you again! You are a holy God, and Israel is supposed to be a holy people. If you are as holy and just as you claim, then you must judge Israel. If you do not judge them, then you are not true to your own nature or your own law. Israel is guilty!"

How do you think Joshua felt during all of this trial? Certainly his heart was broken, his conscience was smitten. What defense did he have?

When you and I have disobeyed God, Satan moves in for that finishing stroke. He attacks us in our heart and conscience. "So you are a Christian?" he sneers. "You are not a very good Christian! You go to church, you read your Bible, you even seek to serve the Lord. And look what you have done! If your friends at church knew what kind of a person you really were, they would throw you out!"

See how subtle and merciless Satan really is. *Before* we sin—while he is tempting us—he whispers, "You can get away with this!" Then after we sin, he shouts at us, "You will *never* get away with this!"

Have you ever heard his hateful voice in your heart and conscience? It is enough to make a Christian give up in despair!

2. SATAN'S WEAPON—ACCUSATION

When Satan talks to you about God, he lies. But when he talks to God about you, he sometimes tells the truth! He is "the accuser of our brethren." He has access to heaven, to the very throne of God; and there he reminds God of the condition of his saints. You and I know about this accusation because we feel it in our own heart and conscience.

"See what Abraham just did! He lied about his wife!"

"Did you see what David did! He committed adultery with his neighbor's wife, *and then killed her husband!* Judge him! Judge him!"

"Were you listening, God? Did you just hear Peter curse and swear and deny your Son three times? Are you going to let him get away with that?"

It is important that we learn to distinguish between Satan's accusations and the Spirit's conviction. A feeling of guilt and shame is a good thing *if it comes from the Spirit of God.* If we listen to the devil, it will only lead to regret and remorse and defeat.

When the Spirit of God convicts you, he uses the Word of God in love and seeks to bring you back into fellowship with your Father. When Satan accuses you, he uses your own sins in a hateful way, and he seeks to make you feel helpless and hopeless. Judas listened to the devil and went out and hanged himself. Peter looked at the face of Jesus and wept bitterly, but later came back into fellowship with Christ.

When you listen to the devil's accusations (all of which may be true), you open yourself up to despair and spiritual paralysis. "My situation is hopeless!" I have heard more than one Christian exclaim, "I'm too far gone—the Lord could never take me back." When you have that helpless, hopeless feeling, you can be sure Satan is accusing you.

3. SATAN'S PURPOSE—
TO BRING AN INDICTMENT BY GOD'S WILL

Satan wants you to feel guilty. He wants you to experience regret and remorse, *but not repentance.* He wants to keep accusing you so that you focus your attention on *yourself and your sins.* If once you look away by faith to Jesus Christ, you will repent, confess your sins, and find cleansing and restoration of fellowship. As long as you are feeling guilty, you are under indictment and you are moving farther and farther from the Lord. True conviction from the Spirit will move you closer to the Lord.

I recall a phone conversation I had with a Christian lady who had lived for several years under the indictment of guilt. She had heard me over the radio and had phoned for help. I do not know her name, but I do know that her case is typical of many Christians.

"When I was a teenager," she told me, "I got into some pretty terrible sin. A few years later, I was saved. Now I'm married and have a family. The other day the pastor asked me to teach a Sunday school class, and I'd really like to, but my past keeps bothering me. I've been asked to teach before, and I've always made some kind of excuse. Do I have to keep doing this for the rest of my life?"

I asked her to get her Bible, and together (over the phone) we read the verses that I will share with you in the next section of this study. It did not take long before she was rejoicing in God's provision for her feelings of guilt. I trust that today she is still serving the Lord.

Satan wants you to feel guilty. Your heavenly Father wants you to know that you are forgiven. Satan knows that if you live under a dark cloud of guilt, you will not be able to witness effectively or serve the Lord with power and blessing. Sad to say, there are some churches that major in guilt. They seem to feel that unless a Christian goes home from a service feeling like a failure, the services have not been a blessing. "Every time we go to church," a lady wrote me, "the pastor spanks us. What should we do?" To be sure, there is a place for proper spiritual conviction; but we must not major on guilt. To do so is to play right into the devil's hands.

Paul had a situation like that in the church at Corinth. One of the members had fallen into sin and had refused to repent and make things right with God and the church. In 1 Corinthians 5, Paul told the church to discipline that man; and apparently they did, for Paul wrote,

Sufficient for such a one is this punishment which was inflicted by the majority. 2 Corinthians 2:6

At first, when this sin was detected, the Corinthian believers were very complacent and re-

fused to act. Paul's letter shocked them into their
senses; but then they went to the other extreme
and made it so hard on the offender that they
would not forgive him! So Paul had to counsel
them,

> so that on the contrary you should rather for-
> give and comfort him, lest somehow such a
> one be overwhelmed by excessive sorrow.
> Wherefore I urge you to reaffirm your love for
> him . . . in order that no advantage be taken
> of us by Satan; for we are not ignorant of his
> schemes. 2 Corinthians 2:7, 8, 11

Excessive guilt and sorrow can only lead to de-
pression, despair, and defeat. Sometimes it leads
to destruction; even Christians have been
known to attempt suicide in order to escape
Satanic accusation.

What, then, is your defense against Satan's
accusations?

4. YOUR DEFENSE—
THE INTERCEDING SON OF GOD

It is true that Satan stands at our right hand to
resist us and accuse us. But it is also true that
Jesus Christ stands *at God's right hand* to inter-
cede for us!

> My little children, I am writing these things
> to you that you may not sin. And if anyone
> sins, we have an Advocate with the Father,
> Jesus Christ the righteous. 1 John 2:1

Our Lord finished his work on earth and returned to heaven to take up his unfinished work. What is that work? Perfecting his children and preparing them for glory.

> Now the God of peace, who brought up from the dead the great Shepherd of the sheep through the blood of the eternal covenant, even Jesus our Lord, equip you in every good thing to do His will, working in us that which is pleasing in His sight, through Jesus Christ, to whom be the glory forever and ever. Amen. Hebrews 13:20, 21

This perfecting ministry has two aspects to it. As our High Priest, Jesus Christ intercedes for us and provides the grace that we need when we are tested and tempted. If by faith we turn to him and come to the throne of grace, he will see us through to victory. But if we yield to temptation and sin, then he ministers as our Advocate to forgive us and restore us to fellowship once again.

> If we confess our sins, He is faithful and righteous to forgive us our sins and to cleanse us from all unrighteousness. 1 John 1:9

Picture once again the courtroom scene in heaven. God the Judge is on his throne. Joshua the high priest stands before God and is dressed in filthy robes. He is guilty. Satan stands at Joshua's right hand to resist him and accuse him. But Jesus Christ is at God's right hand to represent Joshua and to restore him! This explains why Jesus returned to heaven with wounds (not scars) in his body. Those wounds are the everlasting evidence that he died for us. God was merciful and gracious to save us when we first trusted Christ, but he is "faithful and righteous" to forgive us when we confess our sins to him. He is *faithful* to keep his promise, and he is *righteous* or *just* because Christ died for our sins and paid the price of our forgiveness. As sinners, we are saved from wrath by God's grace and mercy. As children of God who have disobeyed him, we are forgiven by God's faithfulness and justice.

Did God close his eyes to the reality of Joshua's sins? Of course not! God will never defend his children's sins—*but he will defend his children*. When Abraham disobeyed and went down to Egypt, and there lied about his wife, God did not defend Abraham's sins; but he did defend Abraham. He kept the ruler from defiling Sarah, and he helped Abraham get out of the land safely. Abraham suffered the consequences of that adventure; for Egypt gave Lot a taste of the world, and this led to Lot's backsliding and downfall. The Egyptian maid, Hagar, that Sarah brought along caused problems in the home and eventually had to be cast out. But God still ruled and overruled to accomplish his purposes with Abraham and Sarah.

When you listen to Satan's accusations, you will focus your attention on yourself and your sins; and this will only lead to defeat and despair. But when you listen to the Holy Spirit's conviction, you will look by faith to Jesus Christ in heaven, your Advocate at the throne of God. You will remember that he died for you and that God cannot reject you, because you belong to Christ. It is because of the heavenly intercession of the Son of God that you and I can defeat Satan's accusations.

Note the stages in the experience of Joshua the high priest. First, there is *Satan's resistance.* The accuser names Joshua's sins at the throne of God and calls for a holy God to judge Joshua. Stage two is *God's rebuke of Satan.*

> And the Lord said to Satan, "The Lord rebuke you, Satan! Indeed, the Lord who has chosen Jerusalem rebuke you! Is this not a brand plucked from the fire!" Zechariah 3:2

Note that God's rebuke of Satan is based on *his grace toward his people.* You and I have been saved by grace. God's grace does not depend on human merit. Jesus Christ went through the fires of judgment that he might pluck us from the burning. Our relationship to God is not based on law or merit; it is based wholly on grace. Grace means that God accepts us in Jesus Christ, not in ourselves.

The third stage is *Joshua's restoration.* God ordered them to remove the filthy clothes and put holy garments upon the high priest. He even put that "holy turban" on his head, the one with the gold plate at the front that read "Holy unto the Lord" (see Exodus 28:36). God did not even put Joshua on probation! He told him to return to the Temple and carry on his service for the Lord!

Resistance—rebuke—restoration: these are

the stages in the experience of confessing sin and returning to fellowship with God. Satan will accuse you, but do not listen to him. Turn by faith to Jesus Christ your Advocate, and confess your sins to him. Depend on what God's Word says, not on how you feel. Rest on the grace of God—he has chosen you, and he will not forsake you. Charles Wesley has put all of this into a beautiful hymn.

Depth of mercy! Can there be
Mercy still reserved for me?
Can my God His wrath forbear,
Me, the chief of sinners spare?

I have long withstood His grace,
Long provoked Him to His face,
Would not hearken to His calls,
Grieved Him by a thousand falls.

Lord, incline me to repent;
Let me now my sins lament;
Now my foul revolt deplore,
Weep, believe, and sin no more.

Still for me the Savior stands,
Holding forth His wounded hands;
God is love! I know, I feel,
Jesus weeps and loves me still.

Unconfessed sin in our lives is a foothold for Satan. He can use that sin as the basis for accusation. The longer he accuses, the greater that sin becomes in our own eyes. It becomes so big that it covers the face of God and hides his grace and his love. We do not experience feelings of conviction that bring us back to God, but feelings of condemnation that convince us that we cannot go back. Guilt becomes in Satan's hands a terrible weapon that destroys our joy, our peace, and our fellowship with God. Our hope fades. We are swallowed up by despair. Then Satan's voice says to us, "Curse God and die!"

Do not listen to the voice of the devil! Instead, listen to the voice of God. Turn to the Word and believe what God says. Rest assured that your Advocate in heaven is waiting to forgive you and restore you. To delay admitting and confessing sin is only to give Satan a greater opportunity to damage your life and ministry.

> He who conceals his transgressions will not prosper, but he who confesses and forsakes them will find compassion. Proverbs 28:13

A REVIEW AND A PREVIEW

We have now met the four persons in the Old Testament who had a personal confrontation with Satan. At this point in your study, it might be a good idea to review the key truths you have learned. The chart on the following page may help you.

In the chapters that follow, I will share other truths about Satan that relate to various areas of life: the home, the church, living by faith, etc. These chapters are based on the material you have already studied. Their purpose is to relate these truths in a practical way to the everyday life and ministry of the believer.

Person	Eve	Job	David	Joshua
Satan's target	the mind	the body	the will	the heart and conscience
Satan's weapon	lies	suffering	pride	accusation
Satan's purpose	ignorant of God's will	impatient with God's will	independent of God's will	indictment by God's will
Your defense	inspired Word of God	imparted grace of God	indwelling Spirit of God	interceding Son of God

FIVE
Living by Faith in God

Everybody in this world lives by faith. The difference between the Christian and the unconverted person is not the *fact* of faith, but the *object* of faith. The unsaved person trusts himself and other humans; the Christian trusts God. It is your faith in God that is the secret of victory and ministry. If you have any doubts that God honors faith in himself, read Hebrews 11. In fact, one of the greatest problems God has with his children is the developing of their faith.

Satan knows this, and therefore attacks the believer's faith. Paul's words to the young Christians in Thessalonica illustrate the point:

> *Therefore when we could endure it no longer, we thought it best to be left behind at Athens alone; and we sent Timothy, our brother and God's fellow-worker in the gospel of Christ, to strengthen and encourage you as to your faith. . . . For this reason, when I could endure*

*it no longer, I also sent to find out about your
faith, for fear that the tempter might have
tempted you, and our labor should be in vain.
But now that Timothy has come to us from
you, and has brought us good news of your
faith and love, and that you always think
kindly of us, longing to see us just as we also
long to see you, for this reason, brethren, in
all our distress and affliction we were com-
forted about you through your faith. . . . as we
night and day keep praying most earnestly
that we may see your face, and may complete
what is lacking in your faith.* 1 Thessalonians
3:1, 2, 5-7, 10

According to Romans 1:17, the Christian is supposed to go "from faith to faith." When you read
the life of Abraham in Genesis 12—25, you see
that all that God did, he did in order to perfect
Abraham's faith. It is a spiritual principle.

"Be it done to you according to your faith."
Matthew 9:29

Whenever God works in and through your life,
it is always in response to faith. The thing that
hinders the working of God is not his lack of
power, but his people's lack of faith.

*And He did not do many miracles there be-
cause of their unbelief.* Matthew 13:58

And He wondered at their unbelief. Mark 6:6

This raises the important question, "How can
the believer *know* that he is living by faith?" It
is so easy for us to be fooled by our own feelings

("But it *seemed right* to do it!") or by the circumstances around us, or by Satan, and his demonic powers. Are there any tests that the Christian can apply to his decisions and actions to determine whether or not he is walking by faith? Yes, there are four practical tests.

Test #1—"Am I doing this for the glory of God, or just to please myself?"

> . . . *yet, with respect to the promise of God, he* [Abraham] *did not waver in unbelief, but grew strong in faith,* giving glory to God. Romans 4:20

Abraham and Sarah were both well past the age of having children, and yet God promised them a son. I think it was F. B. Meyer who used to say, "You never really trust God until you trust him to do the impossible." Abraham begetting, and Sarah bearing a son would certainly be impossible *apart from God.*

> "For nothing will be impossible with God." Luke 1:37

> "With men this is impossible, but with God all things are possible." Matthew 19:26

It was not Abraham's faith in faith that wrought the miracle; it was his *faith in God.* The world's shallow philosophy "Have faith—everything will work out" is as foolish as it is ineffective. Faith in what? Certainly not faith in faith! Abraham and Sarah trusted God, and God performed what he had promised. Because he knew God, Abraham was *fully assured that what He had promised, He was able also to perform.* Romans 4:21

But it is important to notice Abraham's *motive* in all of this: *he gave glory to God.* Faith always gives glory to God, for faith confesses that man is unable to accomplish anything and that only God can do it. Abraham and Sarah were as good as dead physically when they trusted God to work, and this is what brought glory to God.

So whenever you are about to make a decision or take a step in your Christian walk or ministry, ask yourself, "Am I doing this for God's glory alone?" If there is any indication in your heart that self-glory is involved, stop immediately and wait on the Lord for his direction. True faith is motivated only by the desire to glorify God.

Test #2—"Am I rushing ahead impetuously, or am I willing to wait?" We have already learned that faith and patience always go together.

For the Scripture says, "Whoever believes in Him will not be disappointed." Romans 10:11

The quotation is from Isaiah 28:16:

"Behold, I am laying in Zion a stone, a tested stone, a costly cornerstone for the foundation, firmly placed. He who believes in it will not be disturbed" [literally will not be in a hurry].

The Christian who waits for God's leading, and waits on God's working, will not be disappointed or ashamed. True faith is not in a hurry *until*

God opens the way. If you find yourself impatiently rushing ahead of the Lord, beware! You are sure to act in fleshly unbelief instead of in true spiritual faith.

> *. . . and whatever is not from faith is sin.*
> Romans 14:23

Test #3—"Can I defend what I am doing from the Word of God? "True faith is always grounded in the Word of God, the Bible.

> *So faith comes from hearing, and hearing by the word of Christ.* Romans 10:17

No matter how reasonable an action may seem, if it contradicts the Word of God you cannot do it by faith. The Bible gives us precepts to obey, promises to claim, and principles to follow; but if we violate any of these, we are acting in unbelief and not in faith. Our friends may encourage us, and circumstances may seem to favor us (Jonah found a ship waiting for him!). But if we are disobeying the Word of God, we are not acting in faith. This means that God cannot bless us or use us to bring glory to his name.

Test #4—"As I contemplate this move, do I have joy and peace within?"

> *Now may the God of hope fill you with all joy and peace in believing, that you may abound in hope by the power of the Holy Spirit.* Romans 15:13

Where there is true faith, the Holy Spirit is at work; and where the Spirit is at work, he will produce the fruit of hope, joy, and peace. Having the peace of God in your heart is one evidence that you are in the will of God. The peace of Christ is supposed to "rule in your hearts" (Colossians 3:15), and that word "rule" literally means "be the umpire." When you lose God's peace within, you know you have somewhere detoured from the will of God.

It is in this area that the Christian must learn to distinguish between his own human emotions and the deeper work of God in his life. God never denies our emotions; he certainly can use them to accomplish his purposes. But often as we step out by faith, we experience human fears and anxieties; but if we are walking by faith, these fears will eventually be overcome by a deeper joy and peace. This is the work of the Spirit of God in response to our faith in God's Word.

An Old Testament Illustration—Genesis 16. The story is a familiar one. God had promised Abraham and Sarah a child, but the child did not come. As she waited, Sarah became impatient; so she decided to "help God" by having her husband "marry" her handmaid, Hagar. This decision was perfectly legal, but it was not a step of faith. Abraham fell in with the scheme, and the result was trouble.

Now, let's apply our "Four Tests of Faith" to the actions of Abraham and Sarah.

Did Abraham marry Hagar that he might glorify God? No, he married her to please his wife and try to "help God" fulfill his promises.

Were Abraham and Sarah willing to wait? Of course not! That was the whole problem: they ran ahead of God and made a mess out of their home.

Could they base their decision on the revealed Word of God? No, they could not. As you read the life of Abraham, you discover that God blessed and used him whenever he trusted God's Word; but God had to chasten him every time he ran ahead of God's Word. We do not read, "And the Word of the Lord came to Abraham, saying, 'Take your wife's handmaid as a wife and I will give you a son by her.'" Their actions were not based on the Word of God.

Finally, was there joy and peace because of their decision? No, there was misery and war! Hagar fought with Sarah, and Sarah blamed Abraham, and Abraham reasoned with Sarah —until God had to step in and straighten things out. The Jewish nation is still suffering from Abraham's mistake!

Here, then, is a practical home situation that illustrates the importance of walking by faith. Now let's look at

A New Testament Illustration—Acts 27. Again, we have a familiar story. The Roman government had arrested Paul and was taking him to Rome for trial. He and 275 other people were on the ship, which finally arrived at the port of Fair Havens. At this point, Paul (led by the Spirit of God) warned them not to leave port because they would be sailing into danger and destruction.

The centurion in charge, named Julius, had to make a decision: "Do we remain in Fair Havens, or do we set sail?" After considering all the factors, Julius decided to set sail; and the result was just as Paul predicted: the ship was wrecked and it was only by the grace of God that the passengers' lives were saved.

Let's apply the "Four Tests of Faith" to the decision Julius made.

Did he seek to glorify God? No, he did not; in fact, it is likely that he was not even a believer or concerned about God's glory. As you read the chapter, you get the impression that Julius was interested in finishing his task and getting his prisoners safely to Rome as quickly as possible.

Was he willing to wait? No, he was not. He was concerned because already "considerable time had passed" (Acts 27:9), and he would be late arriving at Rome.

Did he base his decision on God's Word? No, he rejected the word that was given through Paul. Instead, he depended on the words of others.

> But the centurion was more persuaded by the pilot and the captain of the ship, than by what was being said by Paul. And because the harbor was not suitable for wintering, the majority reached a decision to put out to sea from there. Acts 27:11, 12

Julius listened to "expert advice" (the pilot and captain), and he took a vote and followed the majority. Then "a moderate south wind came up" (Acts 27:13), and circumstances were just right for sailing! They sailed—but they soon found themselves in a storm, and Paul's prediction came true.

Was there joy and peace because Julius acted as he did? No, there was a violent wind that lasted for two weeks, wrecked the ship, and totally destroyed the cargo. The south wind became a stormy wind; God's Word proved true.

Satan and the "Four Tests of Faith." You have probably noticed that the "Four Tests of Faith" parallel the experiences of the four persons whose confrontations with Satan we have already studied.

David did not act in faith when he numbered the people, because he did it for his own glory and not for God's glory. Pride is an enemy of faith.

Job was tempted to become impatient with God. A willingness to wait on the Lord is an evidence of true faith. Impatience means unbelief.

Eve disobeyed the Word of God when she ate of the tree. True faith is always based on the Word of God.

Joshua had no joy and peace in his heart, because he was suffering under Satan's accusations. True faith brings joy and peace through the Holy Spirit.

This means that you and I must be careful to use the defenses God has given to us. Otherwise, Satan will weaken and discourage our faith and tempt us to stop trusting God. If we seek the glory of God; if we patiently wait on God; if we follow the Word of God; and if we enjoy God's joy and peace within, then we can be sure we are living by faith and defeating Satan.

SIX
Don't Give Satan a Beachhead!

If the believer cultivates in his life any known sin, he is giving Satan an opportunity to get a foothold, a beachhead in his life. Satan will then use this opportunity to invade and take over other areas. Paul warns in Ephesians 4:27, "And do not give the devil an opportunity." The word translated "opportunity" simply means a place such as a city or a building. But it carries the idea of *a foothold or opportunity, a chance to operate.* The J. B. Phillips paraphrase of Ephesians 4:27 reads, "Don't give the devil that sort of foothold." In the language of warfare we would say, "Don't give the devil a beachhead."

It would be well for us to read the entire passage.

Therefore, laying aside falsehood, speak truth, each one of you, with his neighbor, for we are members of one another. Be angry, and yet do not sin; do not let the sun go down on your anger, and do not give the devil an opportunity. Let him who steals steal no longer; but rather let him labor, performing with his own hands what is good, in order that he may have something to share with him who has need. Let no unwholesome word proceed from your mouth, but only such a word as is good for edification according to the need of the moment, that it may give grace to those who hear. And do not grieve the Holy Spirit of God, by whom you were sealed for the day of redemption. Let all bitterness and wrath and anger and clamor and slander be put away from you, along with all malice. And be kind to one another, tender-hearted, forgiving each other, just as God in Christ also has forgiven you. Ephesians 4:25-32

Now, let's consider some of the sins that give Satan a beachhead, and let's try to understand why.

(1) *Lying* (verse 25). Since Satan himself is a liar, it is no surprise that lying opens for him an opportunity to work in our lives (John 8:44). When you believe the truth, then the Holy Spirit can work in your life. When you believe a lie, then the devil can work in your life. We need to heed Paul's counsel in Philippians 4:8:

Finally, brethren, whatever is true, whatever is honorable, whatever is right, whatever is pure, whatever is lovely, whatever is of good repute, if there is any excellence and if any-

*thing worthy of praise, let your mind dwell on
these things.*

Paul gives us a good reason for avoiding deceit:
"we are members of one another." God's truth
builds up the body, but Satan's lies tear it down.
Since we belong to each other, we also affect
each other. If there is deceit in my life, I will
influence you as a member of his body. Since
God is the God of truth, and his Word is truth
(John 17:17), and his Spirit is truth (1 John 5:7),
it is impossible to be in fellowship with God
while you are harboring a lie. Satan tempted
Ananias and Sapphira to lie to God and to the
church, and God judged them severely (Acts
5:1-11). Keep in mind that their sin was not in
keeping back some of the money. Their sin was
trying to make people think they were very
spiritual when in reality they were hypocrites!

Hell is prepared for the devil and his angels
(Matthew 25:41)—and for all liars!

> *But for the cowardly and unbelieving and
> abominable and murderers and immoral per-
> sons and sorcerers and idolaters and all liars,
> their part will be in the lake that burns with
> fire and brimstone, which is the second
> death.* Revelation 21:8

Revelation 22:15 sharpens the focus even more
when it describes deceitful persons as "everyone
who loves and practices lying." In other words,
it is not the person who occasionally lies, for
even the best Christian might do that (Abraham,
for example); but it is the person who makes

lying the love of his life and whose entire life is characterized by deceit. Such a person is so like Satan that he must end up where Satan ends up —in hell.

(2) *Anger* (verse 26). Satan can be angry!

> *"Woe to the earth and the sea; because the devil has come down to you, having great wrath, knowing that he has only a short time."... And the dragon [Satan] was enraged with the woman, and went off to make war with the rest of her offspring, who keep the commandments of God and hold to the testimony of Jesus.* Revelation 12:12, 17

This fact would suggest that anger in our hearts gives Satan a foothold in our lives. And just as lying and murder go together, so anger and murder go together.

> *"You have heard that the ancients were told, 'You shall not commit murder' and 'Whoever commits murder shall be liable to the court.' But I say to you that every one who is angry with his brother shall be guilty before the court; and whoever shall say to his brother 'Raca' [an Aramaic word meaning "empty-headed"] shall be guilty before the supreme court; and whoever shall say, 'You fool,' shall be guilty enough to go into the hell of fire."* Matthew 5:21, 22

To be sure, there is a righteous anger. God expresses anger at sin (Psalm 7:11). Jesus Christ revealed a righteous anger when he drove the religious merchants out of the temple (Matthew 21:12-16) and when he condemned the hypocritical Pharisees (Matthew 23). It is not enough to love the good; we must also hate the evil.

> *Hate evil, you who love the Lord . . .* Psalm 97:10

> *The fear of the Lord is to hate evil.* Proverbs 8:13

> *Abhor what is evil; cling to what is good.* Romans 12:9

However, it is difficult for us as sinful humans to cultivate and exercise a truly *righteous* anger. Our sinful nature has a way of polluting our emotions so that they often do more harm than good. Aristotle said it perfectly centuries ago: "Anyone can become angry—that is easy. But to be angry with the right person, to the right degree, at the right time, for the right purpose, and in the right way—this is not easy."

Sinful anger always leads to more sin. Usually when we are angry, we say things for which later we are very sorry. And often we make decisions that turn out to be hurtful to ourselves as well as others. Satan knows this, so he encourages us to cultivate a sinful anger.

(3) *Stealing* (verse 28). Satan is a thief.

> *"The thief comes only to steal, and kill, and destroy; I came that they might have life, and might have it abundantly."* John 10:10

The experience of two demoniacs of the country of the Gerasenes is a vivid example of how Satan steals from his servants (Matthew 8:28-34; Mark 5:1-20). Satan robbed these men of their sanity, their liberty, their homes (they lived in the grave-yard!), their joy, their effective work in life, their reputations, their health (they cut themselves with stones). And Satan would have robbed them of their lives *and their souls* had they not been set free by Jesus Christ.

Employees who "borrow" things from their employers' offices are inviting Satan to get a foothold in their lives. The person who can steal a fifteen-cent pencil has the potential of stealing a $15 book or a $150,000 payroll!

"He who is faithful in a very little thing is faithful also in much; and he who is unrighteous in a very little thing is unrighteous also in much." Luke 16:10

Note the tense of the verbs: he is already un-righteous, not "he will be."

There is no need to list the various ways that we can steal and try to excuse it. Every man knows his own heart. Some people steal time, others rob God by unfaithful giving (Malachi 3:8 ff.), and still others hold back money that belongs to others (James 5:1-6).

It is interesting to note the reason Paul gives for the believer working and not stealing: that he may be able to give to others! It is our relation-ship to others, not only fear of God's judgment, that helps to govern our lives, "for we are mem-bers of one another" (verse 25).

(4) *Filthy speech* (verse 29). Paul repeats this warning in the next chapter.

And there must be no filthiness and silly talk, or coarse jesting, which are not fitting, but rather giving of thanks. Ephesians 5:4

He is not forbidding holy, healthy humor; the ability to laugh is a mark of maturity and discernment. A leading missionary executive once told me, "I will not send a missionary to the field if he doesn't have a sense of humor." Paul is condemning low humor, jesting that is dirty. This kind of speech tears a person down, and God wants our speech to be "good for edification." Since what we say comes from the heart, impure speech and humor indicates an impure imagination. A person does not have to read pornographic books or see pornographic movies to have a pornographic imagination. If Satan can get us to *think* about sin, and then *talk* about sin, he will have an easier time tempting us to *commit* sin. When we talk freely about filthy things, it takes the edge off our conviction; we get accustomed to it, and soon the barriers are down.

(5) *An unforgiving spirit* (verses 30-32). The believer who harbors bitterness and malice in his heart is giving Satan one of his most effective beachheads! These attitudes (and the others mentioned) hinder the Spirit from working in our lives, and this robs us of the power we need to detect and defeat the devil. The old nature delights in breeding this kind of poison.

The only remedy is forgiveness. If someone wrongs you, forgive him from your heart. Jesus gives simple steps to follow in Matthew 18:15-17;

and he cautions us to be reconciled as quickly as possible (Matthew 5:23-26). The longer you harbor an unforgiving spirit, the more territory Satan will gain in your life. In my pastoral experience, I have seen homes, Sunday school classes, and whole churches weakened and (in some cases) destroyed by Christians who will not forgive one another. Even if the other party does not forgive you, you forgive him. You cannot force him to be forgiving, but you can see to it that Satan is defeated in your own life.

(6) *Slander*—(verse 31; 1 Timothy 3:11; Titus 2:3). Paul commands that the deacons' wives, and the older women of the church, not be "malicious gossips"; this is the Greek word *diabolos*, which is translated "devil." (The word "devil" means "a slanderer, an accuser.") When believers share in gossip and slander, they are doing the devil's work for him and giving him a beachhead for additional work! "You shall not bear false witness against your neighbor" is God's commandment (Exodus 20:16). Among the six things which the Lord hates is "a false witness who utters lies" (Proverbs 6:19).

> *Like a club and a sword and a sharp arrow is a man who bears false witness against his neighbor.* Proverbs 25:18

Slander can hurt a person up close, as does a club, or farther away, as does a sword, or even at a distance, as does an arrow. But whatever the range, the damage is deadly.

Many of the great and godly men of the Bible

suffered because of slander and false witness, including Joseph, David, Jeremiah, Paul, and even our Lord Jesus. Many of the great and godly leaders in church history were slandered by their enemies. It is a painful experience for a dedicated Christian to see and hear his name and ministry maligned, especially when the slander comes from professed believers who pretend to do the Lord's work by exposing the sins of the saints. How Satan must rejoice when he sees Christians slandering each other in print!

The Word of God tells us how to deal with the sins of the saints.

> Brethren, even if a man is caught in any trespass, you who are spiritual, restore such a one in a spirit of gentleness; each one looking to yourselves, lest you too be tempted. Galatians 6:1

> Above all, keep fervent in your love for one another, because love covers a multitude of sins. 1 Peter 4:8

> Hatred stirs up strife, but love covers all transgressions. Proverbs 10:12

This does not mean that love *ignores* sin, or that love *condones* sin. It simply means that love for the brethren keeps us from exposing sin before the eyes of the world and weak Christians; that it keeps us from capitalizing on a brother's fall in order to make ourselves look better. "Don't hang dirty wash out in public," a wise pastor counseled me years ago, and I have found it to be good counsel. I have also found it wise not to believe everything I hear or read about fellow-Christians until there is proof.

Every fact is to be confirmed by the testimony of two or three witnesses. 2 Corinthians 13:1 (See also Deuteronomy 17:6 and 19:15.)

Satan is the slanderer and the accuser of the brethren (Revelation 12:10). When you and I slander the saints instead of praying and seeking to cover the sin in love, we are working for the devil. We should not be surprised if he gets a foothold in our lives and turns our weapons against us!

Any sin that we harbor in our lives, that we know is there and yet we refuse to acknowledge and confess, will give Satan a beachhead for further attacks. It has been my experience that this includes material objects that are definitely related to Satanism and the occult. No Christian has any right to possess such objects because they give Satan the foothold he is looking for. When the Ephesian Christians burned their magic books (Acts 19:18-20), they were taking a giant step forward in defeating Satan.

Finally, we must never look upon any sin or questionable object as "a little thing." Nothing is "little" if Satan can use it to attack you! I recall counseling a Christian student who had an obsession for food. She was ruining her health and her studies, and her anxiety was only making the problem worse. I asked her if she had anything in her possession that was related to the occult. She confessed that she did, and I urged her to get rid of it, confess her sin to the Lord, and claim the victory of Christ over whatever demons were using that object as a beachhead. She did all of this, and the Lord gave her wonderful victory. Illustrations of this kind of victory can be multiplied by pastors who have confronted occult powers.

SEVEN
When Satan Goes to Church

It comes as a shock to some people to discover that Satan goes to church. Through his demonic forces, he is actually *running* some churches! Our Lord cast out demons *in the synagogue,* and Paul wrote to *believers* to warn them about Satan and his devices. Nobody outside the local church can really hinder the ministry of the church; this is why Satan wants to get on the inside, as he did with Ananias and Sapphira (Acts 5).

Where are you likely to find Satan at work in the church?

Let's begin *in the pulpit.* We have already discovered that Satan has "his servants" who "disguise themselves as servants of righteousness" (2 Corinthians 11:15). Simply because a preacher is a professed Christian, a moral man, and a graduate of a seminary does not mean he is truly saved and a servant of Jesus Christ. Saul of Tarsus actually thought he was doing the will of God when he opposed the church; yet he was actually working for the devil.

Of course, Satan also has agents *in the pews.* There are "false brethren" (2 Corinthians 11:26) as well as "false apostles" (2 Corinthians 11:13). The parable of the tares teaches that Satan has "children" and that he sows them wherever God sows true believers. It is easier to become a member of the average local church than it is to join a civic club or a secret order. There was a time when prospective members were carefully interviewed concerning their spiritual experience; but today many churches require only a "profession of faith" and the filling out of the proper forms. What happens when these "children of the devil" become officers in the church? Is it any wonder that churches depart from the faith and start to believe "doctrines of demons" (1 Timothy 4:1).

Satan can be present *in the worship.* I consider worship the most important ministry of the church. Everything the local church does should flow out of worship. Yet in many local churches the congregation is not taught the meaning and importance of worship. The pastor may criticize the "formalism" of a liturgical church up the street and at the same time "produce" the identical religious program every Sunday morning and evening. *Every* church has a liturgy, a form of worship, an order of service. It is either a good liturgy or a bad one. Paul warned the Corinthian church that their lack of order would only make unbelievers think the church members were mad!

If therefore the whole church should assemble together and all speak in tongues, and ungifted men or unbelievers enter, will they not say that you are mad? 1 Corinthians 14:23

For God is not a God of confusion but of peace, as in all the churches of the saints. 1 Corinthians 14:33

But let all things be done properly and in an orderly manner. 1 Corinthians 14:40

Christian worship must be tied to the Word of God and the Spirit of God. The Word of God is the anchor; the Spirit of God is the rudder. God is giving no new revelations; we build our worship on the truths revealed in the Word of God. But God does give new expressions of old truths, and this is where the ministry of the Spirit comes in to guide us. There must be balance and also discernment.

Do not quench the Spirit; do not despise prophetic utterances. But examine everything carefully; hold fast to that which is good. 1 Thessalonians 5:19-21

It behooves the spiritual leaders of the local church to plan the public meetings carefully. Those of us who belong to an independent tradition may criticize the liturgical churches, but we must admit that their liturgy usually shows beauty, content, and balance. It is true that Satan can use dead formalism to kill a church, but he can also use uncontrolled fanaticism.

Christians must also beware of idolatry in worship.

> *What do I mean then? That a thing sacrificed to idols is anything, or that an idol is anything? No, but I say that the things which the Gentiles sacrifice, they sacrifice to demons, and not to God; and I do not want you to become sharers in demons.* 1 Corinthians 10:19, 20

We are prone to assign this warning to the "heathen people" in the dark places of the world, but it applies to the fashionable downtown church as well as the simple neighborhood church. Paul's call for separation in 2 Corinthians 6:14—7:1 emphasizes the incompatibility of Christ and Satan.

> *Do not be bound together with unbelievers; for what partnership have righteousness and lawlessness, or what fellowship has light with darkness? Or what harmony has Christ with Belial, or what has a believer in common with an unbeliever? Or what agreement has the temple of God with idols? For we are the temple of the living God; just as God said, "I will dwell in them and walk among them; and I will be their God, and they shall be My people. Therefore, come out from their midst and be separate," says the Lord. "And do not touch what is unclean; and I will welcome you. And I will be a father to you, and you shall be sons and daughters to Me," says the Lord Almighty. Therefore, having these promises, beloved, let us cleanse ourselves from all defilement of flesh and spirit, perfecting holiness in the fear of God.*

The Corinthian Christians were being invited to attend pagan feasts and to eat food sacrificed to idols. Paul reminded them that the idol was nothing of itself, but that it could be used by the demons to create spiritual problems. There is a true spiritual ecumenicity among the people of God (John 17:20-23); but there is also a false fellowship that seeks to unite Christ and Belial. Of this fellowship we must beware.

Satan can even be at work *in the offering!* The experience of Ananias and Sapphira comes to mind (Acts 5). I also think of our Lord's warning against blowing a trumpet when we give (Matthew 6:1-4).

And what about *the singing?* A seminary professor once told me that "the music was the war department of the church!" Again, we must depend upon the Spirit of God and the Word of God.

> *Be filled with the Spirit, speaking to one another in psalms and hymns and spiritual songs, singing and making melody with your heart to the Lord.* Ephesians 5:18, 19

> *Let the word of Christ richly dwell within you, with all wisdom teaching and admonishing one another with psalms and hymns and spiritual songs, singing with thankfulness in your hearts to God.* Colossians 3:16

It is sad to see congregational worship "in the Spirit" replaced by spectators watching religious entertainment on a church platform. It is even sadder when that "entertainment" presents music that is not biblical. *A singer has no more right to sing a lie than a preacher has to preach a lie!* Satan can lie his way into a church as easily through a song as through a liberal preacher—and perhaps *more* easily! Music plays on the emotions, while preaching touches primarily the intellect and will. There is nothing wrong with emotions in worship, provided they are *true* feelings and not shallow sentiment, and provided they result in a dedicated will that obeys God's Word.

In my conference ministry, I have occasionally had to preach after a "musical number" that was so far from Scripture it could have come from the telephone directory. It is not easy to preach the truth of God's Word after a song that distorted God's Word or refuted it. Alas, even some of the favorite songs and hymns of the church have occasional phrases and stanzas that are simply not biblical; and I believe we should avoid or change them.

Satan often shows up *in the business meetings* of the church too. There is a wisdom from above, but there is also a wisdom from beneath!

Who among you is wise and understanding? Let him show by his good behavior his deeds in the gentleness of wisdom. But if you have bitter jealousy and selfish ambition in your heart, do not be arrogant and so lie against the truth. This wisdom is not that which comes down from above, but is earthly, natural, demonic. For where jealousy and selfish ambition exist, there is disorder and every evil thing. But the wisdom from above is first pure, then peaceable, gentle, reasonable, full of mercy and good fruits, unwaver-

122

ing, without hypocrisy. And the seed whose fruit is righteousness is sown in peace by those who make peace. James 3:13-18

"Earthly, natural, demonic": the world, the flesh, the devil. This kind of wisdom gradually infects a life, or an organization; and before long, Satan is in control. I have participated in many congregational meetings, committee meetings, and board meetings of one kind or another; and I fear that Satan's wisdom has often been present, and some of the believers did not even know it! And, I confess to my shame, on more than one occasion I have been guilty myself.

Satan tries to use leading Christians to spread his destructive wisdom. He even used Peter!

From that time Jesus began to show His disciples that He must go to Jerusalem, and suffer many things from the elders and chief priests and scribes, and be killed, and be raised up on the third day. And Peter took Him aside and began to rebuke Him, saying, "God forbid it, Lord! This shall never happen to You!" But He turned and said to Peter, "Get behind Me, Satan! You are a stumbling block to Me; for you are not setting your mind on God's interests, but man's." Matthew 16:21-23

The legalists who made their speeches in the church council of Acts 15 would have argued that they had prayed about the matter and were speaking the mind of God. Yet they were dead wrong.

Another area where Satan enters the organization of the church is in the selection of *leaders*, including pastors. It amazes me how few local churches really follow the instructions given in 1 Timothy 3 and Titus 1. Few pastoral selection committees investigate the candidate's testimony with those outside the church, or seek to discover whether or not he has financial honesty and integrity. Too many churches put new Christians into places of leadership, instead of giving them opportunity to mature in areas of lesser ministry.

> *... and not a new convert, lest he become conceited and fall into the condemnation incurred by the devil.* 1 Timothy 3:6

Why is it that most churches have to endure a "sanctified obstructionist" who runs everything and has to have his own way? (Alas, sometimes it is the pastor!) Spiritual pride is one of Satan's chief weapons. He loves to lay hold of a Diotrephes "who loves to be first" (3 John 9) and use him to weaken the testimony and, if possible, wreck the church. *There are no seniority rights in the local church.* The fact that a member has been in the fellowship for many years, or in an office many years, is no guarantee of spiritual wisdom. In spite of their immaturity, sometimes the new converts see needs and opportunities more quickly than the older saints.

Finally, Satan tries to work in the church *through an unforgiving spirit.* We have already discussed this in the previous chapter, but it is so important I want to emphasize it. Happy is that church whose members have good memories for God's blessings and bad memories for man's sins. Petty things keep the saints from enjoying one another! An irate woman told me she was never coming back to church because I had not preached a Mother's Day sermon! Another man stopped attending because we re-arranged the order of service and did not open with the doxology. A member "sulked" for weeks because an announcement she wanted made was not included in the bulletin by mistake. Is it any wonder pastors resign? Is it any wonder the machinery of the local church grinds slowly and very little "spiritual product" comes out?

What is the solution? Let every church member—and spiritual leaders in particular—learn to detect and defeat Satan. We must practice "speaking the truth in love" (Ephesians 4:15). We must forgive one another and learn to use the wisdom that is from above. Whenever there is division, we must wait on the Lord for spiritual unity. If unity does not come, we must discover who the people are that Satan is using to hinder the work, and we must deal with them in firmness and love. I know personally how difficult this is, but I also know the blessing and joy that come when Satan has been evicted!

Drive out the scoffer, and contention will go out, even strife and dishonor will cease.
Proverbs 22:10

EIGHT
*What
to Wear
to the War*

It comes as a shock to the new believer that the Christian life is a battleground and not a playground. In my pastoral ministry, I could always tell when a new Christian was starting to mature, because he found himself fighting battles. This was a good sign because, as Spurgeon used to say, "Satan never kicks a dead horse!"

If you are going to win the battle, you must know the enemy, possess power and equipment to attack him, and also have protection against him. In the first four chapters of this book, we met the enemy and learned the strategy that he uses against us. Our power is the Holy Spirit, and we have discovered the spiritual equipment God has given us to attack the devil. It remains now for us to consider the "spiritual armor" that God has provided. It is described in Ephesians 6:10-18.

Finally, be strong in the Lord, and in the strength of His might. Put on the full armor of God, that you may be able to stand firm against the schemes of the devil. For our struggle is not against flesh and blood, but against the rulers, against the powers, against the world forces of this darkness, against the spiritual forces of wickedness in the heavenly places. Therefore, take up the full armor of God, that you may be able to resist in the evil day, and having done everything, to stand firm. Stand firm therefore, having girded your loins with truth, and having put on the breastplate of righteousness, and having shod your feet with the preparation of the gospel of peace; in addition to all, taking up the shield of faith with which you will be able to extinguish all the flaming missiles of the evil one. And take the helmet of salvation, and the sword of the Spirit, which is the word of God. With all prayer and petition pray at all times in the Spirit, and with this in view, be on the alert with all perseverance and petition for all the saints.

Paul emphasizes the fact that the full armor is necessary if we are to defeat Satan. The area in our life that we leave unguarded is sure to be the very place that Satan attacks. On October 17, 1586, Sir Philip Sidney was killed at the Battle of Zutphen, because he was not wearing his full armor. He saw that Sir William Pelham was not wearing leg armor, so Sidney removed his. He was struck in the leg and died from the wound.

I cannot stress enough the importance of *complete* protection.

Let's consider the various parts of the Christian soldier's equipment, and then learn how to put it on and use it.

(1) *The girdle of truth.* Since Satan is a liar, we must oppose him with God's truth. In oriental countries, people wore girdles to bind up their flowing garments and hold everything together. It is God's truth that must hold everything together in our lives. As Christians, we must love truth and live truth.

> *"I have no greater joy than this, to hear of my children walking in the truth."* 3 John 4

The loins are the place of action, mobility, and direction. A soldier with a broken hip would not be worth very much! Unless we are motivated and directed by truth, we will be defeated by the enemy. If we permit any deception to enter our lives, we have weakened our position and cannot fight the battle victoriously.

The girdle of truth is not an offensive weapon; it is for protection. When the believer has what I call "an attitude of truth" in his life, this protects him from Satan's attacks. It does not *prevent* these attacks; it keeps the believer from being harmed by them.

(2) *The breastplate of righteousness.* This piece of armor covered the front of the soldier's body, from the neck to the upper part of the thighs. It protected the vital organs. I believe that Paul is referring here to the righteousness of Christ which we receive when we trust him.

*He made Him who knew no sin to be sin on
our behalf, that we might become the righteousness of God in Him.* 2 Corinthians 5:21

Satan is the accuser, and he attacks us by re-
minding us of our sins. It is through faith in
Christ that we have his righteousness imputed
to us, put to our account. It is important to make
a distinction between *imputed* and *imparted*
righteousness. When a sinner trusts Christ and
is born again, the very righteousness of Christ
is put to his account, and this never changes. As
the believer walks with the Lord and yields to
the Spirit, the righteousness of Christ is imparted to him and he becomes more like Christ.

*. . . and put on the new self, which in the like-
ness of God has been created in righteousness
and holiness of the truth.* Ephesians 4:24

Every believer should know the meaning of the
word "justification." It is the gracious act of God
whereby he declares the believing sinner righteous through the merits of Jesus Christ. Justification never changes. Once God has declared
you righteous, your standing before him is
settled for eternity. However, your state—your
walk—is quite another matter. This changes as
we yield to the Spirit and obey the Word.

It is worth noting that the breastplate covers
the heart, which suggests that our feelings ought
to be protected by Christ's righteousness. Because we *know* we have been accepted by God
and are righteous in Jesus Christ, we need not
fear or fret when Satan throws his accusations
at us. Often Satan will use people—including

Christians—to slander and accuse us; and we are tempted to fight back. But these "fiery darts" (KJV) must not be allowed to penetrate and hit the vital organs. Rest on the finished work of Christ; realize that you are "accepted in the beloved" (Ephesians 1:6, KJV); and know that God's righteousness, imputed to you, will never be removed.

(3) *The shoes of peace.* Roman soldiers wore hob-nailed shoes for stability and mobility. How you stand pretty well determines how you will fight. If a fighter loses his footing, he may lose the battle. The Christian with solid footing is going to have confidence as he faces the enemy. He is also going to be able to respond to Satan's various attacks should the enemy change his strategy.

We stand because of the gospel. We know that

> *Christ died for our sins according to the Scriptures, and that He was buried, and that He was raised on the third day according to the Scriptures, and that He appeared . . .*
> 1 Corinthians 15:3-5

It is this victory of Christ that gives us a safe and solid standing as we fight the devil. Wherever we walk, we stand on victory ground!

> *Therefore having been justified by faith, we have peace with God through our Lord Jesus Christ, through whom also we have obtained our introduction by faith into this grace in which we stand; and we exult in hope of the glory of God.* Romans 5:1, 2

131

The word "preparation" (verse 15) means "equipment, readiness." It means that the believer is prepared for the devil's attacks. He stands, and therefore he is able to fight. His Savior has already won the victory, and he stands in that victory.

Paradoxical as it may seem, the Christian soldier wages peace, not war. He fights Satan that he might bring peace. Satan is the cause of sin and unrest and division in the world. The Christian soldier wages peace by opposing Satan. The gospel message is one of peace, but it is a declaration of war as far as Satan is concerned.

(4) *The shield of faith.* The Roman shield was two feet by four feet, made of wood covered with leather and metal. It served as a movable wall behind which the soldiers could hide and protect themselves from the burning arrows shot by the enemy. It is your faith in Christ that quenches these fiery darts. Just as much as you trust him, you will share his victory.

What are the "fiery darts" (verse 16, KJV) that Satan shoots at us? I take it that they are thoughts of one kind or another—doubts, fears, worries, and so on. I have sometimes been prayerfully meditating on the Word when suddenly a terrible thought would invade my mind. Of course, Satan wants us to think that *we* are to blame, because this kind of thinking would make us discouraged with our Christian walk. But *he* is to blame! I have had fiery darts thrown at me while I have been preaching the Word! If we do not quench these darts, they will ignite whatever they touch, and we will have a destructive fire to put out.

I have found that *trusting God's promises* and laying hold of his Word will quench these fiery darts. How important it is for the Christian soldier to know Bible doctrine! (This explains why the Christian soldier is described in chapter 6 of Ephesians. Paul spends the first three chapters explaining basic doctrine, and the next two on basic Christian living.) We do not quench the darts by faith in ourselves (even our past victories), faith in faith, or faith in some creed. It is faith in Christ and his Word. We cannot stop Satan from throwing the darts, but we can keep them from starting a fire. A great saint has said (was it Martin Luther?), "I cannot keep the sparrows from flying about my head, but I can keep them from making a nest in my hair!"

The important thing is to *quench that dart immediately*. Instantly look to Christ by faith, recall some promise of the Word, and believe it. Otherwise the fire will start to spread, and if you add fuel to it it will get beyond your control. Your feelings will get aroused and upset, and before long Satan will be in control.

I can recall situations in which fiery darts made me impatient, and I was about to say and do things for which afterward I would have been sorry. I turned to the Lord in faith and believed him for the patience I needed. There came to me a sense of control and calm that quenched the fiery darts. The times I have *not* turned to him in faith, I have been burned—and so have others.

(5) *The helmet of salvation.* We should certainly relate this to 1 Thessalonians 5:8:

. . . and as a helmet, the hope of salvation.

I think Paul is here referring to the hope the believer has in the return of Jesus Christ. Satan often uses discouragement and hopelessness as weapons to oppose us. It is when we are discouraged that we are the most vulnerable. We will make foolish decisions and be susceptible to all kinds of temptations. When the mind is protected by "the blessed hope" of the Lord's return, Satan cannot use discouragement to attack and defeat us.

Discouragement is a lethal weapon in the hands of the enemy. Moses and Elijah became so discouraged they asked God to kill them. The psalms record some of the occasions when David was "in the depths" and could only hope in God.

Why are you in despair, O my soul? And why are you disturbed within me? Hope in God, for I shall again praise Him, the help of my countenance, and my God. Psalm 43:5

When your mind and outlook are focused on the return of Christ, it protects you against the despair and discouragement that always come to the life of dedicated believers. When Paul was in his final imprisonment, facing certain death, forsaken by many of the believers in Rome, he encouraged himself with this hope:

In the future there is laid up for me the crown of righteousness, which the Lord, the righteous Judge, will award me on that day; and

not only to me, but also to all who have loved
His appearing. 2 Timothy 4:8

(6) *The sword of the Spirit.* This is an *offen-sive* weapon; the other parts of the armor are for *defense*.

> *For the word of God is living and active and*
> *sharper than any two-edged sword, and pierc-*
> *ing as far as the division of soul and spirit,*
> *of both joints and marrow, and able to judge*
> *the thoughts and intentions of the heart.*
> Hebrews 4:12

The spiritual sword of the Word of God is differ-ent from any material sword that man may wield. A material sword gets dull with the using, but the Word of God remains sharp. A material sword must be handled by physical power, but the spiritual sword already has life and power in it. The Spirit of God enables us to use the Word of God effectively! Our Lord used the sword of the Spirit when he met and defeated Satan in the wilderness temptations. "It is written!" he said, and he quoted the Old Testament Scriptures. Martin Luther knew this lesson well, and he wrote about it in his great hymn, "A Mighty Fortress is Our God."

> *And though this world, with devils filled,*
> *Should threaten to undo us;*
> *We will not fear, for God hath willed*
> *His truth to triumph through us.*
> *The prince of darkness grim,*
> *We tremble not for him;*
> *His rage we can endure,*

> *For lo, his doom is sure!*
> *One little word shall fell him!*

I have dealt with the use of the Word of God in Chapter One, and you may want to review that section.

Putting the armor on. All of this is just so much Christian symbolism unless you know how to put the armor on; and the answer is in Ephesians 6:18. I am giving it in a literal translation.

> *By means of every prayer and supplication for your need, praying at all times, in the Spirit, and keeping alert with all perseverance . . .*

George Duffield caught this truth in his familiar gospel song, "Stand Up, Stand Up for Jesus."

> *Stand up, stand up for Jesus,*
> *Stand in His strength alone;*
> *The arm of flesh will fail you—*
> *Ye dare not trust your own.*
> *Put on the gospel armor,*
> *Each piece put on with prayer;*
> *Where duty calls, or danger,*
> *Be never wanting there.*

We put on the armor by means of prayer, and we pray by means of the Holy Spirit.

My own experience has been that the morning devotional time is the best time to put on the armor. After I have given God my body, mind, and will (see Section 4 of Chapter Three), I ask the Holy Spirit to fill me; and then I *by faith* put on the pieces of the armor. I pray something like this:

"Father, thank you for the provision you have made for victory over Satan. Now, by faith, I put on the girdle of truth. May my life today be motivated by truth. Help me to maintain integrity. By faith, I put on the breastplate of righteousness. May my heart love that which is righteous and refuse what is sinful. Thank you for the imputed righteousness of Christ. By faith, I put on the shoes of peace. Help me to stand in Christ's victory today. Help me to be a peacemaker and not a troublemaker. By faith, I take the shield of faith. May I trust you and your Word today and not add fuel to any of Satan's darts. Thank you that I can go into this day without fear. By faith, I put on the helmet of salvation. May I remember today that Jesus is coming again. Help me to live in the future tense. Protect my mind from discouragement and despair. By faith, I take the sword of the Spirit. Help me to remember your Word and to use it today. Father, by faith I have put on the armor. May this be a day of victory."

This is not a routine prayer, and I have not recorded it here so that you can memorize it and repeat it. Rather, it is here to give you some idea of how we put on the pieces of the armor by faith, by prayer. This is a private matter between you and the Lord. I cannot tell you *how* to pray; but I can tell you that you had better pray!

Paul describes the kind of praying we must do. It is *persevering* prayer—"praying at all times." It is not enough to mumble a few pious words at the beginning of the day. This kind of praying will never defeat Satan.

> *"Now he was telling them a parable to show that at all times they ought to pray and not to lose heart."* Luke 18:1

> *"Pray without ceasing."* 1 Thessalonians 5:17

This does not mean that we go around saying prayers under our breath. It means that we are in a constant attitude of prayer and trust, that the receiver is off the hook so to speak.

It is also *balanced* prayer—"all prayer." What is "all prayer"?

> *Be anxious for nothing, but in everything by prayer and supplication with thanksgiving let your requests be made known to God.* Philippians 4:6

"All prayer" involves worship, adoration, confession of sin, supplication, thanksgiving. If all we do is ask for things, we will miss the true blessing of balanced praying. Prayer that is only asking can be selfish praying. It takes "all prayer" to defeat Satan.

It is also *Spirit-empowered* praying. We must pray "in the Spirit." This means that the Spirit must reveal to us *what* we should pray about, and that he must empower us to keep on praying. *True prayer is not easy.* If we pray in the energy of the flesh, God will not answer. We will give up before long, and Satan will win the victory.

Finally, it must be *watchful* praying. "Be on

the alert." No soldier can afford to close his eyes to the enemy. (By the way, the prayer posture of closing the eyes, bowing the head, and folding the hands is not found in Scripture. The Jews prayed with their eyes open toward heaven and their hands lifted toward God.) "Watch and pray" was our Lord's repeated admonition to his disciples (Mark 13:33, 14:38). Be alert to what the devil is doing, or he will attack you while you are praying!

D. L. Moody did not encourage his songleader Ira Sankey to use the familiar song, "Onward Christian Soldiers." Moody felt it was not true to experience. "The church is a poor army," he said. We are indeed "a poor army," because we do not use the equipment God has provided for us. God commands us to stand and withstand! And he enables us to do it!

Put on the gospel armor,
Each piece put on with prayer.

NINE
Satan's Army

Since Satan is a created being, he is not like God in being all-knowing, all-powerful, and everywhere-present. (Theologians call these attributes omniscience, omnipotence, and omnipresence.) Satan appears to be omnipresent because he has a demonic army assisting him in his warfare. There is only one devil, but there are many demons. There are some basic facts you need to know about demons.

THEIR ORIGIN

Skeptics try to tell us that there are no such beings as demons, that this whole idea is but a remnant of ancient myths and superstitions. But if we accept the authority of the Bible, we must believe in the existence of demons. The Lord Jesus believed in demonic forces and often delivered helpless people from their power. Jesus taught that there was a definite enemy named Satan, and that he ruled over a kingdom of evil beings. Since Jesus came "to bear witness to the truth" (John 18:37), we must believe that what he said was truth and not merely accommodation to the superstitions of the people.

It seems likely that demons are the angels who revolted with Lucifer and fell with him (Isaiah 14:12-15; Revelation 12:3, 4). Jesus spoke of "the devil and his angels" in Matthew 25:41. Nowhere does the Bible teach that demons are the spirits of the wicked dead returned to earth, or that they are the spirits of some pre-Adamic race.

The description given of demons certainly tallies with what we know of the character of Satan. Demons are *"unclean spirits"* (Matthew 10:1). They encourage people in moral filth. Certainly the frightening increase in pornography and sex worship is due to the activity of demons. They are called *wicked spirits* (Matthew 12:45). Apparently there are degrees of wickedness among the demons. It is not difficult to believe that demons are behind the wickedness mankind is committing today. They are also called *evil spirits*. This word *evil*, according to the Greek lexicon, carries the meaning of "base, worthless, vicious, degenerate." Satan himself is called "the evil one" (Matthew 13:19). If you want to know the depths to which these evil beings can lead a man, read about the two demoniacs in Mark 5:1-20.

It is interesting to note that the demons have faith in God.

You believe that God is one. You do well; the demons also believe, and shudder. James 2:19

Demonic faith is certainly something less than saving faith! The demons believe that Jesus Christ is the Son of God (Luke 8:28), and that there is a future judgment awaiting them (Luke 8:31). They always feared when Christ or one of his servants came on the scene.

THEIR ORGANIZATION

Satan is a destroyer and a divider when it comes to the church; but in his own kingdom, he is very well organized. Please do not get the idea that Satan today is reigning in hell and that all of his agents are sent forth from the pit. Satan is the "prince of the power of the air" (Ephesians 2:2), and he "prowls about like a roaring lion" on the earth (1 Peter 5:8; see Job 1:7). His army is busy, assisting him in his battle against God and God's people.

Jesus called Satan "the ruler of the demons" (Matthew 12:24). Paul described Satan's hierarchy in Ephesians 6:12.

For our struggle is not against flesh and blood, but against the rulers, against the powers, against the world forces of this darkness, against the spiritual forces of wickedness in the heavenly places.

This is the picture of an organized kingdom, an organized army.

Daniel 10:13 indicates that Satan has special

angels assigned to the nations of the earth. The answer to Daniel's prayer was delayed because God's angel had a battle with "the prince of the kingdom of Persia." This account reveals the importance of prayer in the accomplishing of God's will in this world, and also the opposition of Satan when the believer prays.

Satan and his hosts are organized. If only believers could be united in their defense and their warfare, Satan would not win so many victories. Sad to say, Christians too often are so busy *fighting one another* that they have no time for fighting the devil. As Lord Nelson said to two officers who were quarreling, "Gentlemen, there is but one enemy—and he is out there!"

THEIR OPERATION

Like their master, demons are deceivers and destroyers (John 8:44). Not all sickness is demonic. Jesus commissioned his disciples to "heal the sick ... cast out demons ..." (Matthew 10:8), making a distinction between the two. But demons can cause physical affliction. They can make people *dumb* (Matthew 9:32), *blind* (Matthew 12:22), and *crippled* (Luke 13:11). They can *torment* people (Matthew 15:22), and even drive them to *suicide* (Matthew 17:14 ff.). There is no question that some bodily affliction is caused by demons.

But like their master, demons seek to deceive. They are the teachers of false doctrine (1 Timothy 4:1 ff.). They are the promoters of the occult and various forms of divination (Acts

16:16-18); and they are the force behind idolatry (1 Corinthians 10:14-22). Satan has always wanted to be worshiped, and the demons lead unsuspecting men to satisfy Satan's desire.

Demons work through people. This is why Paul instructs us not to fight against "flesh and blood." Satan works in and through unsaved people (see Ephesians 2:1-3), but he can also work in and through saved people. Remember Peter (Matthew 16:21-23) and Ananias and Sapphira (Acts 5). The Christian soldier needs to be alert at all times.

The word translated "demon-possessed" (Matthew 4:24; 8:16, 28, 33; 9:32; 12:22; 15:22) simply means "demonized." I do not know of any Scripture that explains the relationship between the demons and the person who is demonized. We know the results and we know the cause, but we do not know the details of the relationship between the two. Certainly demons can take control of a person who yields himself to them. If there is some unclean thing in a person's life, this gives the demons a foothold.

Can demons "possess" a Christian? Theologians debate the issue. I have a feeling that the problem lies with the definition of "possess." What does it mean to be *demonized*? How extensive is the *possession*? I have personally discussed the question with reputable Christians who have confronted demons in the lives of believers. One of my missionary friends has had considerable experience in this area. If the flesh can still work in a believer who is indwelt by the Spirit, so can the devil. Perhaps the terms "demonic influence" or "demonic obsession" would be better than "demon-possession."

However, this much is true: demons can and do influence and use people who are saved. While we have no precedent in the Bible for *casting* demons out of saved people, we do have precedent for *fighting* demons who seek to influence saved people. Ephesians 6:10-18 was written to Christians.

If the demons cannot succeed in luring us to the grossly unclean things of sin, they will move to "higher ground" and their temptations will be more subtle. After all, Satan "disguises himself as an angel of light" (2 Corinthians 11:14). He uses *religion* to ensnare people! Morality without the righteousness of Christ is one of his chief traps for catching and holding lost people. The drunkard, the dope addict, the thief, all know that they are sinners; but the self-righteous church member is convinced that he is a saint.

THEIR OUTCOME

An incident and a parable from the life of Christ help us answer the question, "What will happen to Satan and his army?"

> Then there was brought to Him a demon-possessed man who was blind and dumb, and He healed him, so that the dumb man spoke and saw. And all the multitudes were amazed, and began to say, "This man cannot be the Son of David, can he?" But when the Pharisees heard it, they said, "This man casts out demons only by Beelzebul the ruler of

the demons." And knowing their thoughts He said to them, "Any kingdom divided against itself is laid waste; and any city or house divided against itself shall not stand. And if Satan casts out Satan, he is divided against himself; how then shall his kingdom stand? And if I by Beelzebul cast out demons, by whom do your sons cast them out? Consequently they shall be your judges. But if I cast out demons by the Spirit of God, then the kingdom of God has come upon you. Or how can anyone enter the strong man's house and carry off his property, unless he first binds the strong man? And then he will plunder his house." Matthew 12:22-29

Christ invaded Satan's kingdom when he came to this earth as a man. Satan, of course, knew that he was coming, and he did all in his power to prevent it. Satan even tried to kill Jesus after he was born. When he invaded Satan's kingdom, Christ also overcame Satan's power. "The strong man" came face-to-face with One who is stronger! In his life, death, and resurrection, Jesus Christ has completely overcome Satan's power. Today he is claiming the spoils. He is rescuing sinners from Satan's dominion and then using those changed lives to defeat Satan's forces! Like David who slew Goliath and then used the giant's own sword to cut off Goliath's head, Jesus Christ defeated Satan and is using the spoils in his own warfare. Jesus "led captive a host of captives" (Ephesians 4:8), and those captives became soldiers of the Lord.

Satan, then, is a defeated foe, and he knows it.

His "mystery [secret program] of lawlessness" is being restrained by the Holy Spirit working in and through the church (2 Thessalonians 2:1-12). When the church has been raptured to heaven, and Satan is cast out of heaven, he will have a short time on earth and will destroy everything he can (Revelation 12). But his doom is sure: he and his angels will be cast into a place of eternal fire (Matthew 25:41; Revelation 20:1-3).

The dedicated Christian wants to avoid two extremes when it comes to the matter of demons: (1) seeing a demon behind every tree; and (2) treating the doctrine of demons with disdain or contempt. The first attitude leads to fanatical fears, the second to false security. Both are dangerous. If you practice the principles given in this book, you will understand the workings of the demonic forces, and you will be able to detect and defeat them. Jesus defeated demons by the Spirit of God (Matthew 12:28), and so may we.

"Greater is He who is in you than he who is in the world." 1 John 4:4

TEN
Satan and the Home

The first attack Satan made was against the home. He invaded Eden and led the first husband and wife into disobedience and judgment. Satan is still attacking the home. This does not mean that all wrecked homes are the fault of Satan, for often the flesh has a lot to do with the problems. If a Christian marries out of God's will, the enemy can have a field day in that home. If either or both partners are too immature for the demands of marriage, Satan can find openings for subtle (and not so subtle) attacks. If the married couple does not obey the Bible and leave father and mother, but instead permits the parents to interfere, then Satan has an easy time attacking that marriage.

But there are some specific areas of attack mentioned in the Bible, and these must be noted by Christians who are married.

(1) *Satan teaches doctrines that forbid marriage.*

> *But the Spirit explicitly says that in later times some will fall away from the faith, paying attention to deceitful spirits and doctrines of demons, by means of the hypocrisy of liars seared in their own conscience as with a branding iron, men who forbid marriage . . .* 1 Timothy 4:1-3

Our Lord makes it clear in Matthew 19:12 that not everyone is supposed to get married. Some people are hindered from marriage because of birth, perhaps some physical problem. Others cannot marry because of the responsibilities men have placed upon them; and still others must remain single in order to serve God better. (Paul was apparently in the last category.) Singleness is a Christian option; but for most people, marriage is the will of God. However, Satan's approach is to convince the person that *marriage is sinful.* He wants us to believe that the single state is more spiritual than the married state, and this idea, of course, is false. The whole cult of celibacy and virginity is based on this doctrine. To be sure, there are those people whom God has called to a life of celibacy; it is a gift from God (1 Corinthians 7:7). But you must be sure this is the will of God and not a deception from Satan. Any teaching that claims greater spiritual virtues and blessings for the celibate than for the married is of the devil and not from God.

(2) *Satan seeks to reverse the headship in the home.*

> *Let a woman quietly receive instruction with entire submissiveness. But I do not allow a woman to teach or exercise authority over a man, but to remain quiet. For it was Adam who was first created, and then Eve.*
> 1 Timothy 2:11-13

> *Wives, be subject to your own husbands, as to the Lord. For the husband is the head of the wife, as Christ also is the head of the church, He Himself being the Savior of the body.*
> Ephesians 5:22, 23

Headship is not dictatorship. Headship is leadership in love. Christ is the Head of the Church in a living, loving relationship; and so the husband ought to be the head of the wife in a living, loving relationship. Please note that the subjection of the woman is *not subjugation.* Man and woman are made out of the same basic material, and they are one in Jesus Christ (Galatians 3:28). Satan almost destroyed the first home by separating Eve from her husband at a time when she needed his spiritual leadership. Eve operated independently from her husband, then led him into sin.

This is not to suggest that husbands are more spiritual than their wives. They ought to be, since they are the spiritual leaders in the home; but often they are not. But wise is that dedicated Christian woman who encourages her husband in the things of the Lord and helps him be a better spiritual leader in the home.

(3) *He wants to lead husbands and wives into moral impurity.* I read somewhere that 50 percent of the married couples admit that one partner of the other has been unfaithful. Usually these affairs have been passing experiences, not repeated; but they have had in them the seeds of all kinds of problems in the home. This is why Paul wrote,

> *Now concerning the things about which you wrote, it is good for a man not to touch a woman. But because of immoralities, let each man have his own wife, and let each woman have her own husband. Let the husband fulfill his duty to his wife, and likewise also the wife to her husband. The wife does not have authority over her own body, but the husband does; and likewise also the husband does not have authority over his own body, but the wife does. Stop depriving one another, except by agreement for a time that you may devote yourselves to prayer, and come together again lest Satan tempt you because of your lack of self-control.* 1 Corinthians 7:1-5

Several principles emerge from this important paragraph. First, sex in marriage is not sinful, and there must be a mutual understanding that governs the intimate life of the Christian couple. We are not supposed to "use" each other selfishly. Second, abstinence is permitted for spiritual reasons; but do not put yourself into a place of temptation. Satan is so subtle that he can tempt a Christian man who is praying! Marriage is one help to self-control in the area of sex.

It has been my experience as a pastor that the husband and wife who are considerate of one another, and who fulfill their marriage dues, will not be interested in any other man or woman. Satan knows when husbands and wives are robbing each other, and he arranges for extramarital opportunities to gratify the normal desires of the body. Husbands and wives who use sex as a weapon to fight with instead of a tool to build with are asking Satan to wreck their home.

(4) *He gets the wife too busy outside the home.* According to 1 Timothy 5:9-16, the early church had an organized program for assisting Christian widows. There were, of course, no government agencies or welfare programs in that day. The widows had to qualify before the church would accept them. Paul counsels the younger widows

> to get married, bear children, keep house, and give the enemy no occasion for reproach; for some have already turned aside to follow Satan. 1 Timothy 5:14, 15

The yielded Christian wife should find joy and fulfillment in her home. Christian girls who are not interested in bearing children, keeping house, and caring for a husband simply should not get married. They will only make themselves and the man they married miserable. Granted, there may be situations where the husband and wife get along happily disregarding this biblical injunction; but I cannot help but feel that they are losing something in their relationship.

Be that as it may, Satan is anxious to get the wife away from the home and interested in exciting experiences apart from her husband and family. This kind of temptation is especially dangerous to the gifted wife who has abilities she can barter in the business world. I am not saying that it is wrong for a wife to work outside the home. I am saying that both the husband and wife had better be alert to Satan's temptations. When *outside the home* is more inviting and exciting than *inside* the home, then you can be sure Satan is at work to wreck that marriage.

It is a serious thing to be a husband or wife, a father or mother. God holds the husband responsible for the spirituality of the home (read Ephesians 5:18 ff.). Satan attacks the husband and father, seeking to lead him out of the will of God. Satan also attacks the wife and mother. This is why Christian couples need to read the Word and pray, not only individually but together as a family. Invariably when a Christian counselor confronts a family problem, he discovers that the husband and wife have stopped praying and reading the Word together.

Your home needs the same spiritual defenses as the individual: the inspired Word of God, the imparted grace of God, the indwelling Spirit of God, and the interceding Son of God.

FOR ADDITIONAL INFORMATION

There are many books available on the subject of Satan, demons, and the occult. Some of them are sensational; some are truly biblical. I can sincerely recommend the following:

The Christian Soldier and *The Christian Warfare* by Dr. D. Martyn Lloyd-Jones (Baker Book House). Dr. Lloyd-Jones is a master expositor who knows the human heart as well as he knows his Bible. These two volumes expound in detail Ephesians 6:10-20.

Angels, Elect and Evil by Dr. C. Fred Dickason (Moody Press). This is the best doctrinal treatment of this subject I have ever seen. Dr. Dickason has had wide experience in dealing with demons. He writes from the perspective of both a theologian and a practical counselor.

The Adversary by Mark I. Bubeck (Moody Press). Pastor Bubeck has had an unusual ministry in detecting and defeating demonic forces.

This is an excellent companion volume to Dr. Dickason's book.

Demons In The World Today by Dr. Merrill F. Unger (Tyndale House). Dr. Unger is too well-known as a theologian and writer to need any endorsement from me! He has some later books out which you will want to read, but this is his basic text on the subject.

The Voice of the Devil by Dr. G. Campbell Morgan (Baker Book House). There are only four sermons in this brief book, but they are weighty! If Dr. Morgan had included David and Joshua in his series, I would not have written this book.

The Invisible War by Dr. Donald Grey Barnhouse (Zondervan). Any book from Dr. Barnhouse is worth reading, and this one especially. He traces the whole conflict between Lucifer and Christ as recorded in the Bible. When I first read this book, I could not put it down until I had completed it.

Between Christ and Satan and *Occult Bondage and Deliverance,* both by Dr. Kurt Koch (Kregel Publications). The author is a student of the occult, has traveled widely, and has interviewed believers who have had personal dealings with demons. Dr. Koch's books (and I have not listed all of them) are for the more advanced student, so do not move ahead too rapidly. Be sure you have a solid foundation first.

Satan, His Motives and Methods by Dr. Lewis Sperry Chafer (Zondervan) is an old standard that was written before the rise of the modern Satan movement. It is good for exposition of basic doctrine.

Let me issue a warning here: *it is a dangerous thing to be "curious" about Satan and the occult.* Do not dabble in doctrine. Recognize the fact that Satan and his hosts will begin to attack you as you grow in your knowledge of their secrets. Either devote yourself to a life of battle and victory, or decide to stay behind the lines.

The above books are not listed in any special order of importance. The fact that a book about Satan is not included does not mean it is not worth reading; there are just too many of them to list.